the
mac &
cheese
millionaire

erin wade

the mac & cheese millionaire

building a better business by thinking outside ☐ the box

WILEY

Published by John Wiley & Sons, Inc., Hoboken, New Jersey.
Published simultaneously in Canada.

Author disclaimer: This book is the true telling of my wild ride through entrepreneurship. To keep the story from being long and confusing, some stuff is skipped, other stuff condensed, and some characters merged so that instead of following the trajectory of three different kitchen managers over a decade, you can just follow one. Some names have been changed to protect people's privacy, while others have been changed to prevent people described as jerks from suing me (I mean, they are jerks after all). Just to really throw you off, some names (hi Kate!) have not been changed at all. I did my best to re-create scenes and conversations as faithfully as possible, but anyone who has ever been to couple's therapy knows that there are always multiple interpretations of the same events, so take it with a grain of salt that these are my memories and impressions. I hope you enjoy them.

For general information on our other products and services or for technical support, please contact our Customer Care Department within the United States at (800) 762-2974, outside the United States at (317) 572-3993 or fax (317) 572-4002.

Wiley also publishes its books in a variety of electronic formats. Some content that appears in print may not be available in electronic formats. For more information about Wiley products, visit our web site at www.wiley.com.

Library of Congress Cataloging-in-Publication Data

Names: Wade, Erin, 1981- author. | John Wiley & Sons, publisher.
Title: The mac & cheese millionaire : building a better business by
   thinking outside the box / Erin Wade.
Description: Hoboken, New Jersey : Wiley, [2024] | Includes index.
Identifiers: LCCN 2024025039 (print) | LCCN 2024025040 (ebook) | ISBN
   9781394264438 (hardback) | ISBN 9781394264452 (adobe pdf) | ISBN
   9781394264445 (epub)
Subjects: LCSH: Small business—Management. | Small business—Planning. |
   Corporate culture.
Classification: LCC HD62.7 .W38 2024 (print) | LCC HD62.7 (ebook) | DDC
   658.02/2—dc23/eng/20240702
LC record available at https://lccn.loc.gov/2024025039
LC ebook record available at https://lccn.loc.gov/2024025040

Cover design and illustration: Wiley

SKY10081013_080524

For Elena, Ellie, Eliza, and Isaac

I hope this book helps you find joy and purpose on your own unique journeys. Thank you for being the most fulfilling part of mine.

Contents

Introduction

I am the world's leading expert on macaroni and cheese. A bold claim, I realize—but it's the God's honest truth.

I have personally cooked more than 10,000 mac and cheese dishes. I have grated over one metric ton of cheese, boiled thousands of pounds of pasta, and whisked such vast amounts of cream sauce that I developed a wrist injury my doctor told me she has only seen in teenage boys with masturbatory addictions.

I wrote the global best-selling cookbook and definitive work on the topic, creatively titled *The Mac and Cheese Cookbook*. Amazon ranks it as the 65,739th most popular book of all time, placing it just above *Tanya's Comprehensive Guide to Feline Kidney Disease* (#175,890), and just below *Fifty Shades of Grey* (#25,370).

I built a cult macaroni and cheese restaurant, Homeroom, which has sold millions of mac and cheeses over a decade in business. Homeroom's mac and cheese is so popular that it has been featured everywhere from the *Wall Street Journal* to the Cooking Channel, and its financial performance puts it in the top 1 percent of restaurants nationwide. Put simply, no one has dedicated more of their life to this cheesy carb than I have.

You might be wondering, why the hell would anyone spend so much of their life focused on macaroni and cheese? (Or, if you're really into mac, perhaps you are not wondering this.)

I went down the rabbit hole of dairy-filled obsession for the same reason most people do crazy things: for love.

Not for the romantic love of another, but for another kind of love we don't talk about nearly as much—because I wanted to love who I was at work. I would hear people talk about being excited to wake up in the morning to go to work, and I thought they were crazy—that maybe I just wasn't that kind of person. I wanted to love who I was in the world and how I spent my days there. I wanted the people around me to feel the same way.

At the time I decided that I wanted to open a macaroni and cheese restaurant, I was living what I had been *told* was a fairytale ending. I had graduated from top schools and was working as a highly paid lawyer in a cushy high rise in San Francisco. I sounded important at cocktail parties, looked damned respectable in a suit each day, and did work representing some of the largest companies in America. The problem was that I was miserable. I had won at playing a game I didn't even like, but had labored over perfecting for most of my life.

Opening Homeroom in 2011 was my personal Hail Mary to fall in love with work. I hoped that the longing I felt for something more meaningful could be found in making delicious food and sharing it with people. And while that proved to be true, I ended up loving my work not for any of the reasons that I articulated at the outset. While I began Homeroom out of a love of macaroni and cheese, what I ultimately fell in love with was business. And specifically, how you can create a business that centers on meaning, purpose, and connection.

Over the decade I led our team at Homeroom, I began to define success differently than the fairytale I had been raised with. I became obsessed with picking apart the reasons that other jobs and workplaces sucked, and how to do better. Through an embarrassing amount of trial and error, my team and I developed language and systems that maximized meaning, purpose, and connection, and created a more suck-free workplace. In an industry where the average tenure of employees is fewer than 90 days, Homeroom's average was 2.5 years. And if I can practice hippie-dippy ideas in a business where the profit margins are notoriously abysmal, where failure rates are the highest of any industry, and that attracts entry-level, minimum wage labor, then I believe these ideas can work almost anywhere.

I decided I wanted to write this book after two important things happened: my Homeroom team changed the world, and I was given a large heap of money. I know that the first one sounds grandiose, but in our case it's actually true. Or at least as true as companies that lay claim to world-changing but that make things like internet browsers.

In response to an incident at Homeroom, my team used all the tools we had come up with over the years to put together an anti-harassment system that became the subject of a viral op-ed I wrote in the *Washington Post* and was subsequently adopted by the Equal Employment Opportunity Commission and restaurants around the world. The system we came up with virtually eradicated harassment at our restaurant and has the potential to significantly improve the lives of the one in ten Americans who work in hospitality. I didn't share our system in a public way for many years because I thought my business was too small and unimportant to be worthy of national attention. This experience of using my voice to effect important change made me wonder what kind of improvements are possible when business is done differently, and when women and smaller-scale leaders use their power and their voices. I wrote this story to encourage others to do the same.

As for the heap of money, after ten years in business, Homeroom's stellar performance attracted the attention of a high-powered restaurant group that purchased the company in a multimillion-dollar deal practically unheard of for a small dining establishment. It was just like a Disney movie, except if the princess was a scrappy, off-beat business and the prince a large corporate conglomerate. (Note to Disney: when you realize the American public is ripe for such a capitalist love story, the rights are available.) I retained a seat on the board of directors, as the only woman, and one of the few members without access to a private plane. Slowly, I started to expand my focus from how to build my own career and company to how to use what I had learned to help others on their path. I wanted to write this book to give to other people the language I wish I had been given to understand my own dissatisfaction at work and the tools to create something more compelling.

I also wanted to write this book because a huge part of my success was embracing my competitive advantage as a woman, and I believe there are valuable lessons for people of all genders in talking openly about that. Most business books look a lot like the board room I currently occupy—exclusively white, male, and from gigantic companies. And while I love a tech bro in a hoodie as much as the next gal, there are a lot of people like me for whom the masculine norms of business simply don't resonate. If so, this book is for you.

Mine is a story for anyone who has ever loved their work, or would like to. It is about the spark that is passion, and what happens when it is given fuel to become fire. It is about how to find connection, meaning, and purpose, even in unlikely places. It is about commitment, and what it takes to sustain the long-term relationship that is a career. It is also about macaroni and cheese.

1

Passion

The Best Fuel Out There, Other Than Chocolate

"I have no special talents. I am only passionately curious."

—*Albert Einstein*

When I was little, my family made pilgrimages from our low-slung home in the San Fernando Valley to a seafood shack in Malibu that was the highlight of my week. I loved this place because they fed you unlimited free peanuts while you were waiting for a table, and you could throw the shells on the floor. Reveling in behavior that would have been deviant elsewhere, I stomped on the discarded peanut shells with my feet while we were waiting. After being seated, I proudly ordered a heaping bread bowl of fresh clam chowder even though it was only 10 a.m., and clams don't come from the ocean in Malibu.

Afterwards, I ran down to the beach and played in a storm drain, which I lovingly called "the river." I spent many happy hours playing there, building sandcastles in the runoff that led to the sea. The beach was adjacent to a deafening highway, and I was literally frolicking in sewage—but I didn't care; we were at the ocean! The salt in the air lent it a wild quality, and the sun always seemed a touch brighter there. Every time we crested the hill overlooking the sea on the drive to Malibu a huge grin spread across my face. Such was the magic of the ocean to me.

Twenty years later, I crested a hill to a different part of the Pacific. That same smile overtook my face when I caught a glimpse of the deep blue expanse. I was exhausted from middle-of-the-night feedings for my second child and the brilliant idea that I had to demonstrate my commitment to work by not taking maternity leave.

Somewhere between 2 a.m. feedings and 2 p.m. meetings, the world had constricted. The small universe I had chosen to occupy meant doing a lot for my kids, my partner, and my colleagues, but didn't leave much space for me.

Then one morning, a tiny ball of energy began flickering in my chest. It called me to the ocean. I decided to pay attention and signed up for a surfing class the same day. I arrived in Pacifica, a sleepy surf town south of San Francisco, and met my instructor. His eyes were bloodshot and I could detect the faint odor of weed on his clothing, but working moms with limited free time can't be choosy, so out we went.

For those of you with images of warm, sunny, welcoming California beaches, let me clarify: what you're picturing is a postcard from Southern California.

In Northern California, the icy water streams down from Alaska so the beaches are frigid, with more down-jacket than bikini weather. The region is known as the "Red Triangle" because it is the world's largest great white shark breeding ground, and most beaches offer up just as much rock as they do sand. In short, getting in the water at Pacifica was about as glorious as that Malibu storm drain.

I loved it.

I splashed around in the crumbly waves, trying my best to catch something. I laughed deep belly laughs every time the instructor tried to get me on a wave, and I tumbled off the board into the foamy whitewater. Even though I was failing miserably at the sport I was there to learn, every time the crisp, salty water washed over my face I felt invigorated, alive.

The ocean woke me up, and not just because the water was 53 degrees. It was the first time I had done something motivated by pure joy, just for the fun of it, for as long as I could remember. Flailing my middle-aged mombody around in a freezing cold ocean guided by a stoned 19-year-old was just what the doctor ordered.

After the lesson, I impulse-bought the longest surfboard that would fit in my car (in my newbie enthusiasm, the innovation of a surf rack had not occurred to me) and made a promise to myself. No matter what happened, for the next year I would go to the ocean once a week and try to surf. And I did.

We think that this is part of what it means to grow up, to be mature. We do what we should do instead of what we are called to do, and in the process lose touch with the very core of ourselves.

I didn't ride a real goddamn wave for that first year, but it was a joy to be in the water. The following year, I increased my promise to myself to twice a week. Following an obsession with YouTube tutorials, I actually started surfing real waves. That was a joy, too. The following year I increased my promise to surf three times a week. And I did.

When I told people about this promise to myself, they were always impressed. Inevitably they would point to something that they had tried to do, like going to the gym every week, that had failed. The thing that no one seemed to understand—the thing that was at the heart of my promise—is that it's not work when you genuinely want to do something. This was something I craved, not a choice to do something that someone else like a doctor or a fitness magazine thought I should do but that I didn't really want to do. I was propelled to the beach weekly not out of a sense of duty, but by my own motivation to experience something I desired deep within. I did it not for sculpted arms, or a lower heart rate, or because someone else might think it looked cool. I did it just for me.

Life has a way of training us out of paying attention to the part of ourselves that acts from a place of pure passion. The part of us that likes to play in the storm drain just because it's fun. When we think of how we will spend our days, or pay our bills, we are taught to look toward the practical. What skills can we learn that will be most marketable? What items on our résumé will look impressive? What kind of salary will pay for a house? This is like my friends who complain that they never want to go to the gym. Why? Because the gym sucks, and someone else told them they should go. We think that this is part of what it means to grow up, to be mature. We do what we *should* do instead of what we are called to do, and in the process lose touch with the very core of ourselves.

I didn't become a surfer because I looked around and made a practical choice. I became a surfer by following a passion that was sparked in a storm drain decades ago and followed it where it took me. I reignited the spark even though I had let it burn down long ago, and I rekindled it until the spark became a blazing fire.

2 | Failure

The Shittiest Part of Finding Success

"Knowing what you can *not* do is more important than knowing what you can do. In fact, that's good taste."

—*Lucille Ball*

As a kid, I loved playing soccer. My parents, busy, self-employed wards of three children, tried to combine activities for us whenever possible to minimize pickups and drop-offs, so they signed up my brother for soccer as well.

My brother Stephen is not exactly what you'd call a natural athlete. He inherited the stocky, Eastern European build of my mom's Jewish roots, and all the crappy genetics that go along with it. If we both ate a salad, he would gain a pound of water weight while I would lose that same amount. His spotty vision required glasses from a young age, which, coupled with his love of Shakespeare, gave birth to his nickname: "The Professor." He had to wear a corset-like brace for years to correct the scoliosis in his back and was best known in social circles for his dead-on impressions of Julia Child, who was also his most frequently chosen costume for Halloween.

My brother hated going to soccer and complained about it endlessly. He was only five at the time, but he pulled out all the stops. He feigned illness, "lost" his cleats before practice, and threw epic temper tantrums. When none of this worked, he pulled out the pièce de résistance. In the middle of a game, in the burning heat of the midday LA sun, he lay down in the middle of the field and stopped moving.

In family lore, there is much disagreement about what exactly he said to register his disapproval. The top contenders are "Take me out, Coach!" and "I just can't take it anymore." Regardless, everyone on the sidelines screamed for him to get up. The other players narrowly avoided him as the play swirled around him frantically. But he didn't get up. He remained steadfastly glued to the ground, staring up at the sky, until the coach pulled him out at the first opportunity. That was Stephen's last soccer game.

For me, getting fired was sort of like that.

At the time, I was working as a corporate lawyer. Like Stephen, I didn't like the game I was playing. My office was sandwiched between one lawyer who routinely punched our shared wall when angry, and another who thought it appropriate to take the summer associates to strip clubs. (Our firm represented companies that got sued for doing dumb-ass things like taking summer associates to strip clubs.)

For those of you who have been fortunate enough never to inhabit that world, here's how it works: success is defined by how much time you bill to clients, which is measured in six-minute increments. There is a minimum number of hours you must bill every year, with substantial bonuses for billing more. What is measured is not quality, efficiency, or even whether you win your cases, just how much time you can put on the clock each day, how many dollars out of clients' pockets. It is deeply inspiring work.

There is something inherently demoralizing about going to work each day knowing no matter how quickly you draft a brief, how efficiently you run a meeting, or how high the quality of your work product, you still need to sit at your desk the whole damn day, measuring your time every six minutes. If you want to know why cat videos were invented, it was for people doing exactly this kind of work.

My boss Kiki was permanently bronzed from frequent visits to a local tanning center, donned impossibly high heels, and had Fergie's "Glamorous" as the ringtone on her cell phone. She billed more hours than the next three partners combined and had clawed her way to the top of the legal world from a poor, working-class upbringing where little was expected of her. I might have admired her for it, if she wasn't also a complete asshole.

One day, I was sitting at my desk nursing a mug of tea and billing my fourth increment of six minutes to a client when my phone rang. Kiki wanted me to research an urgent legal question. I opened the research program on my computer and began scanning for relevant cases.

My phone rang again a minute later. "Have you found an answer yet?" Kiki asked.

"No," I answered.

"Well," she huffed, "that's disappointing." With that, she hung up.

I turned back to my browser and tried not to feel rattled. Another minute later, my phone rang again.

"Do you have it?" she asked.

"No," I replied.

"Did you go to law school?" she cried. Click.

I began to sweat, knowing another call would be on its way shortly, and I had barely even signed into the research program.

My phone rang again. "So?" she asked.

"I'm sorry—not yet," I replied.

We continued this charade for 20 minutes.

Eventually, I told Kiki that her calls on the minute were preventing me from finding the answer she was so desperately seeking. She made a sound like a dying cat on the other end of the receiver, and then hung up on me again. I wasn't sure how to interpret that strangled feline noise, but pressed on. She stopped calling.

She didn't even use the research until about a week later, at which point I had already been terminated. Not for this transgression, but for generally not giving a fuck.

To be fair to my former employer, if you have a player who doesn't want to play the game, you should kick them off the team. I am not even sure that I made the same overtures my brother had made at soccer. I showed up to my legal career by lying down on the field. I didn't want to cater to the whims of partners at all hours of the day and night, so I didn't. I didn't want to bill the maximum number of hours each year in six-minute increments, so I left my desk the second I hit my hours quota each week. I was the last one to volunteer to stay late, or work weekends, or take any interest in anything beyond the bare minimum possible to skate by. It turns out companies don't want to pay you a lot of money to do that. And, frankly, they shouldn't.

My secretary, Maria, 20 years my senior, offered to take me out right after they terminated me. She bought me a fancy hot dog with spicy mustard on top and tried to give me a pep talk. "One day you'll look back on this moment as the best thing that ever happened to you," she said.

I was fighting an oncoming migraine and trying to appear as though I was not moments away from erupting into tears. "I hope you're right," I said, stuffing an oversized bite of hot dog into my quivering mouth.

I had never been fired from anything in my life, and even though I hated my job with the burning rage of a thousand hells, it felt like being dumped by a girlfriend I didn't even like. Which is to say, pathetic.

I felt ravaged inside, not because I had failed at being a lawyer but because I had failed at something much more significant. I was living a life not of my own making, and not even trying to play a game I didn't care about.

I had picked a law school because it was pass/fail, so I could do as little as possible to get my degree. I spent most of law school not even showing up to classes, and instead getting really good at yoga and perfecting my bagel recipe. I convinced friends to tutor me right before finals, which was often the only time I set foot in the classroom all semester.

The thing is, this wasn't who I was, or who I wanted to be. I'm the kind of person who went to summer school all through high school because I wanted to learn about things that my school didn't offer, like photography. I wrote stories for the fun of it and won a screenwriting award for a story I penned in my free time in high school. I learned to cook by volunteering at a restaurant while I was an undergrad. I like learning. I like working. But I didn't like the work I was doing.

> *I felt ravaged inside, not because I had failed at being a lawyer but because I had failed at something much more significant. I was living a life not of my own making, and not even trying to play a game I didn't care about.*

It turns out that when you don't like the work you do, you're very likely to suck at it. And there is nothing worse than sucking because you don't even care. I had been lying on the field for quite some time, begging for someone to notice and pull me out of the game. They finally did, and I was benched to contemplate my losses. My boss was responsible for pulling me out of that game, but it was my turn to choose whether or not to get back on the field.

3

Termination

Why Being "Let Go" Is the Best Euphemism Ever for Losing Your Job

"Courage is what others can't see, what is never affirmed. It is made of what you have thrown away and then come back for."

—*Leonard Cohen*

Have you ever thought about the phrase "being let go," instead of "being fired" or "terminated"? *Terminated* sounds like your life is actually being put to an end. Being *fired* conjures being engulfed by flames, so that's also like your life is being put to an end, but this time in the most painful way possible. Both of these phrases have a covert implication that losing your job is tantamount to being extinguished as a human being.

To be "let go," by contrast, sounds downright delightful. As if your old job set you free to greet something else that was calling you. Like being released into the embrace of something more beautiful.

The morning after I lost my job (another ridiculous phrase, like "oops—where did it go?!"), I definitely felt like I had been fired. My insides felt like they were burning, as acid roiled in my gut at the thought of calling my family to share the news. I decided to hit the road for a few days to clear my head. I'd call my family from the car.

My parents were going to freak out. My mother, like many Jews of her generation who lost family in the Holocaust, is obsessed with financial security. My grandparents were the sole survivors of large families all killed by the Nazis, so my mother grew up without grandparents, aunts and uncles, or extended family. Instead of weekends playing with the cousins, she was raised on stories of acute loss from the Old Country. If you want to know what kind of effect this has on the psyche of Jews, look no further than your average Jewish garage. Growing up, I did not know a single Jew without a second refrigerator tucked away in the garage. Instead of a second car, Jews would opt for the second fridge. You never know when you might have to run for your life, so make sure there is plenty of kugel for the apocalypse. For people with two refrigerators in their home so they don't run out of food, a family member being out of work is like a nuclear event.

"Oh no!" my mom said when I broke the news. "How could they do this to you? Those schmucks. Do you want me to call my friend Esther, the lawyer in Boca, to see if she has any leads?"

I think this is a Jewish thing—when a crisis hits, the answer always seems to be to call another Jew who is tangentially related to see if they can help. This person is usually either a cousin eight times removed, or an "aunt" who is not really related to you but shared a scrap of bread with your

15

grandmother at Auschwitz that one time. I've always hated this system, because usually the person cannot offer any meaningful help, but they'll always try to do something, which usually results in me having coffee with some poor schmo who also can't help but is a Jew, and therefore willing to show up for a coffee obligation with a total stranger.

"No thanks," I said, "I'm not sure that a retired lawyer ten states away is going to help with my search here. I'm not sure I want to go back to that, anyway."

"What do you mean you're not sure you want to go back to that?" my mother asked.

"I really didn't like my job" I replied. "I'm not sure I want to get another one like it."

My mother sighed. "You see, this is what's wrong with your generation. No work ethic. You think you're supposed to enjoy working. That's why they call it *work*, and they don't call it *fun*! I'll call Esther and give you a call right back." My mother clicked off.

I stared at the road and, in an attempt to avoid my own thoughts, decided to keep calling people. To counterbalance the effect of my mother's disappointment, I called my best friend Kate, a native Michigander who has the upbeat countenance only a non-Jewish Midwesterner can have.

She picked up on the first ring. "Hey there!" she said, "You feeling better about being freed from the worst job of your life?"

I paused and thought about it. "I'm not actually sure that was the worst job of my life. There was that summer I spent working at the flower store, where my boss had cameras everywhere and watched us from home. That was pretty creepy."

"Fair enough," Kate said, "the second worst job of your life."

"Oh! And then that summer where I worked at a factory applying labels to linen packages in the 100-degree heat. That was pretty awful, too."

"Okay," Kate said, "the third worst job of your life."

The more I started thinking about it, the less sure I was that I had ever had a job I would describe in a positive manner. When people said they enjoyed getting up to go to work in the morning, I worried that maybe they were just a different kind of person. Like Kate was just made of different stuff than my mom. More positive stuff.

"So what's next?" asked Kate.

"I feel crazy even saying this out loud," I admitted, "but I keep coming back to restaurants."

"Really?" said Kate. "I thought you were done with that."

"Not working for other people, but opening my own."

"Ooh, now you've got me interested," she said.

I had been mulling it over for months. I'd come home one night from the office in the pouring rain with a pounding headache, craving a bowl of macaroni and cheese and a good old-fashioned couch-sit. I had perused the take-out menus of practically every restaurant in Oakland before I realized that there was no restaurant I could go to that would make the dish I was craving. What I wanted was my dad's mac and cheese, and I had yet to visit a restaurant that could make it as good as he did.

My dad cooks exactly four and a half things: macaroni and cheese, chocolate chip cookies, brownies, pancakes, and chicken à la king (which is just the sauce for mac and cheese with peas and chicken added, poured over rice—so really a variation on dish number one). Although that's all he's got in the bag, all of these dishes are the very best version of those foods you will ever eat. So when I was craving my dad's mac and cheese, no other recipe would do.

Even though I wanted to fall onto the couch and binge-watch *The Sopranos,* I dragged my body to the market to get the ingredients. I set about grating the cheddar and whisking the cream sauce until it was silky and smooth. The steam from the final dish flushed my cheeks, and the warmth of the bowl felt good in my hands. I took a bite and closed my eyes. The sharp tang of the cheese, the silky richness of the sauce, and the rounded simplicity of the elbow noodles took me back to a much simpler time in life. I licked the bowl clean.

In that moment, I realized how rare it is to enjoy a food where my version is the most delicious one I've ever tasted. Yet there wasn't a single restaurant dedicated to it. There are pizza restaurants, burger joints, BBQ places; why was there no place to go to for mac and cheese that night? I couldn't stop thinking about it.

"You know," I said to Kate, "I tried to scrape together the money before I went to law school to open my own bakery but couldn't quite swing it. I did that underground wedding cookie business, which was fun. I feel like I've been circling the wagon for years but haven't taken the leap."

"I thought restaurants were too crazy for you." Kate responded.

"Well, they are too crazy when I'm working for other people. The work is repetitive. The hours are long. The bosses are unhinged. Maybe if I was the boss, it would be different."

"How different?" asked Kate.

"I'm not sure. I feel like I've always wanted to do my own thing. I feel like I'm in this little window right now where I don't have a house, don't have any kids.. . .I don't know if and when I'll have this kind of freedom again. I just don't want to go back to being a lawyer."

"Well," said Kate, "then you shouldn't. This is the only life you've got. If you feel like you'll always wonder if you don't try this, then why the hell not? What's the worst that happens?"

"I lose all my money," I said. "I'll have no house, no savings, no nothing. I'm also afraid of looking like a complete idiot."

"Anyone who would judge you for trying for your dream isn't worth your time anyway," said Kate. "And don't you think you could make more money by being a lawyer again if you had to?"

"I suppose so," I said, despite my doubts.

"Well, then your worst-case scenario looks exactly like your default scenario if you don't try it, so why wouldn't you go for it?"

I had never thought of it in that way. She was right. I had settled in my career for my default worst-case scenario and was thinking about doing it again. I had picked something that would pay the bills but not engage me on any other level. That option would always be available—a safety net I could return to. When had I decided not to leap toward greatness and instead just plopped directly into the safety net?

In the days and months that followed, I realized that I hadn't been terminated, nor fired. I had indeed been let go, and I would learn from this freedom and use it wisely.

I began telling my family and chosen family about my plan. When you have practiced a profession for only half as long as you were in school studying to do it, people start to worry that you're unstable. When you practice a profession for only half as long as you were in school studying it and then leave it to open a macaroni and cheese restaurant, people will *know* that you're unstable.

Here's what my mother said when I told her the news: "Are you kidding me?! You're almost 30. Why don't you save up a bit more, have a few kids, and do this in like ten years when you're a bit more stable?"

"You think in ten years when I'm stable with a few kids I would gamble it all on a restaurant?" I replied. "I don't think that'll ever happen."

"Well I think this is insane," my mom said. "You could be a Supreme Court Justice and you're going to give it all up to cook macaroni and cheese."

"Mom, I don't think I was ever going to be a Supreme Court Justice. I had crappy grades in law school and never even clerked for a judge."

"Well," my mom said, "I could've been on the Supreme Court, and I'll always regret it. I don't want you to make the same mistake."

"Mom, you're a speech therapist," I replied.

"You know what I mean," she said.

"No, actually I don't," I said.

Well, this was going well. I paced my kitchen and started fidgeting with a loose cabinet handle.

"Erin," my mother continued, "you are so fortunate to have a stable profession—why don't you just cook for fun like other people do. Go buy one of those fancy pizza ovens and put it in your backyard?"

In the days and months that followed, I realized that I hadn't been terminated, nor fired. I had indeed been let go, and I would learn from this freedom and use it wisely.

"Mom, I hate my work, and I don't think that making pizza on the weekend is going to fix that."

The cabinet handle broke off the door and fell to the floor with a clang. My mother was undeterred by the commotion.

"What do you hate about being a lawyer?" she asked.

"Everything—it's so destructive," I replied. "The entire premise is that people fight with each other, and you help them do it. Each side comes at it from the most selfish place possible, trying to slowly bankrupt the other both financially and morally, and then somehow you hope that this broken system leads to justice. Only it generally doesn't because the side that wins is frequently the one with either more money or worse ethics—and they push the other side into submission. I can't imagine a more depressing way to spend my days. I'd rather build something for a living rather than constantly destroying things."

My mother paused while I collected the handle from the floor and placed it on my windowsill. Perhaps this was beginning to sink in for her.

"Then why not be a judge?" she countered.

Oy.

"Mom," I replied, "that takes years to do. And then you are just a referee of this awful game instead of a player in it. I don't see how that's much better. And also, you started your own businesses—why do you think it's so disgraceful if I do the same?"

"See, I could never argue with you," she said. "That's why you're such a great lawyer. You know, your grandparents survived the Holocaust and moved to America to give the next generation a better future. We have given you every opportunity and this is what you're going to do with it? I can't believe you're going to throw your life away like this."

"You think I'm throwing my life away?" I asked.

"Yes, I do," she replied.

Buoyed by the loving encouragement from my family, I pressed on.

4 | Dreams

Sometimes Scary, Always Interesting

"Hope is a very unruly emotion."

—*Gloria Steinem*

"Mmm...I like it."

At one year old, those were my first words. I was sitting in a high chair, being fed spoonfuls of vanilla custard, and my tiny taste buds were so excited I was moved to speak for the first time. In a sentence, no less.

Food was a daily adventure in my childhood, a way to explore without going anywhere. In elementary school, I packed my own lunch full of American junk food to trade with the first-gen kids in my class whose parents had meticulously packed them delicacies from their home countries. I traded Doritos for kimbap, Korean sushi filled with a rainbow of vegetables like crunchy pickled daikon sprinkled with sesame seeds. I offered up Oreos in exchange for a warming chicken curry served in a tiffin, courtesy of my friend's Indian mother. I gobbled Mexican cemitas—spicy pork sandwiches on a fluffy bolillo roll in exchange for my Capri-Sun.

I have no idea why my parents asked no questions when I sent them to Costco as a seven-year-old requesting nothing but processed junk food to pack as my school lunch, but all I can say is that it was a different time. As long as I was growing, didn't ask them to make lunch for me, and didn't have scurvy, it was a win.

It's funny how we all crave what we don't have. For my friends whose parents cooked, all they wanted was American junk food. All I wanted was a lovingly homemade meal.

I also wanted something approximating adventure. My public elementary school campus consisted of a large, dreary building with bars on the windows and concrete covering every surface. There were no trees to climb, no grass to run on. When we had school meetings, we were counted off and marched out like little soldiers and were told to greet the principal in unison. "Good morning, Mrs. Tyler," we would chirp—our only opportunity at interaction being as one unified body, by the hundreds.

When I felt lost, or I was somewhere I didn't want to be, I could count on food to reconnect me with myself. For some people, this happens through meditation. For others, religion. For me, barbecued pork. I'd take a bite of my friends' lunches, close my eyes, and my body would light up, chronicling the different flavors and textures.

To get to why I wanted to open a restaurant, I need to rewind the tape to a time before I ever became a lawyer. While I could trace it to those first

23

words in that high chair, or my elementary years of enterprising lunch swaps, the first moment it occurred to me that I could make a living through my obsession with food came lying in bed with my college girlfriend. I am embarrassed to admit it, but it was her idea.

"I'm so excited about the show I'm directing," she exclaimed. "You're gonna come to the opening next weekend, right?"

"Of course," I said, "How could I miss it?"

"Fabulous," she said, "I'm so glad you'll be there."

I turned my face to meet hers. "I'm so proud of you—it's so invigorating to be around you doing something you love so much. Your energy is downright infectious."

"Thanks, babe," she said. "So, what's bringing you energy these days?"

I thought long and hard. "Sandwiches," I replied.

"Sandwiches?" she said.

"Yep, sandwiches. I've been thinking about everyone's obsession with the chicken pachanga sandwich at Hoagie Haven."

"And?" she asked.

"I mean, first off, what the hell is a chicken pachanga anyway?" I asked.

"I don't know," she replied.

"But secondly, Hoagie Haven is such a long walk from campus, and that sandwich has so much liquid in the form of ranch and hot sauce that it's always soggy by the time I eat it. I can't help but wonder if they layered the chicken and perhaps the lettuce differently, that it could protect the bread from the sauces while in transit."

She paused. "Erin, we're lying here naked and what's on your mind is the saucing of a chicken pachanga sandwich?"

"It is."

"Girl, I adore you. But have you ever thought that instead of doing something academic maybe you should just do cooking? Like, as a job? You never want to talk about school, but you talk about food the way I talk about theater."

No one had ever asked me that question. I didn't know you could do cooking as a job. A chef is not a doctor, lawyer, or banker—the only three professions recognized by the Jewish religion—and so it had never occurred to me. The term "celebrity chef" had yet to be coined, and there was scant media programming about food. Restaurants were not where upstanding people went to make it; they were where misfits went to support their drug addictions.

I decided to learn how to cook, and that the best way would be to offer up my useless services for free in exchange for knowledge. Who would turn down free help, even if that help was not actually very helpful?

A week later, I walked into the fanciest restaurant in town—one that I had been dying to eat at when my parents came to town since I could not possibly afford it on my own. It had a masculine, old-school quality, with starched tablecloths, hunter green wallpaper, overstuffed leather chairs, and dim lighting.

I arrived in the middle of the afternoon, as the kitchen staff were noisily banging away. The owner, a bald, red-faced man, answered the door. He took my hand in his large, rough palm, and shook it firmly. "How can I help you?" he asked.

"I've admired your restaurant from afar," I said, "and was wondering if I could work for free in your kitchen to learn more about food."

"Have you ever eaten here?" he asked.

"No," I replied, sheepishly. "I can't afford it," I confessed. "But I was going to ask my parents to bring me here for graduation."

"Hmm," he said. "Well, that's ballsy. Do you want to try it?"

"Um, yeah, I would love that."

He walked back toward the kitchen and half-opened the swinging door. "Nick! Fire a squid," he yelled. "Take a seat," he told me.

He poured himself a drink and offered me one. It was 2 p.m. He shared a story about the kitchen where he learned to cook, and the burn he got on the third day that was so deep it left a scar he still carries. He talked about how he spends half of his time living on a boat in the Caribbean near his other restaurant, and how the women there make it hard to leave.

The squid arrived. It had been sliced into the thinnest of rings, then fried in an airy batter. The exterior crust shattered upon the lightest touch and had a pleasant grit from flecks of cornmeal. The squid itself was juicy and tender, with a slight but pleasant chewiness that allowed it to linger in my mouth for a few extra seconds before being swallowed.

"You seem like a nice enough kid," he said. "You can come learn from our crew. How do you like the squid?"

My face lit up. "Mmm...I like it."

5 | Apprenticeship

Fake It Till You Make It

"What one has not experienced, one will never understand in print."
—*Isadora Duncan*

The first soccer team I ever played on was at age five, in a Jewish soccer league named after the famous warriors in the Hanukkah story. They combined the boys and girls on the same team, and my Israeli coach, Chaim, spent the games muttering expletives under his breath in Hebrew and keeping all the girls on the bench.

While boys and girls eventually develop differently as athletes, at age five they are functionally the same. No one is very strong, very coordinated, or knows what the hell they are doing. The style of play resembles a swarm of honeybees chasing a sugar cube.

That being said, I was good. Very good. Like, didn't always swarm the ball kind of good. Neither of my parents knew anything about soccer, but I had asked them if I could be on a team because I had picked up playing soccer against the boys on the schoolyard in kindergarten and was running circles around them.

The sidelines of the Jewish soccer league were packed with a smattering of different kinds of anxious people—mothers wringing their hands calling out for their sons to be careful, and fathers desperately wanting their sons to be the best and punctuating their incessant pacing with cries of encouragement. "You've got this Yoni—get it to the goal!"

Chaim's eyes would dart across the field while he yelled instructions to the boys. "Spread out," he would cry. "Pass it to Levi!" He studied their actions and corrected their behavior, every moment an opportunity for them to get a little bit better while the girls stagnated on the bench. My hands tucked solemnly in my lap, I waited for an eternity to be asked to play.

While the boys were lavished with Chaim's attention and attendant foul language, I quietly seethed, itching to show off what I could do. When he did put me in, always in the game's final minutes, I would run as fast as I could, my little legs burning, hoping that if I showed him how good I was, he would let me play more. He never did.

The following year, my parents moved me to a regular all-girls league, where I finally got to play and emerged as a star. As an adult, I would occasionally wonder what would have happened if I hadn't moved to that team. Instead of becoming a high-level player who honed her skills through practice, I would barely have touched the field. Instead of seeing myself as the leader I ultimately became, I would have presumed I was second-rate, barely worthy of my spot.

And not because I couldn't have achieved at the level of the boys, but merely because I didn't conform to the image of what the men in charge understood a soccer player to be—namely, a younger version of themselves.

While this realization is depressing as hell, it turns out that my experience with Jewish soccer was a useful harbinger of what was to come later in life. Whether in professional kitchens, as a lawyer, or as a businessperson, I was often one of few women in the room, trying to convince men in charge that I could be a real asset if only they would let me play.

The first of these experiences was at my *stage* (French for unpaid kitchen labor) at the fancy French restaurant in Princeton, New Jersey. The men (and they were all men) in the kitchen were a mix of large, burly Irish guys who were always drinking and small, quiet Mexican workers diligently prepping. The grill was the size of my torso, and there were eight burners on the range, two deep fryers, a broiler, and an oven. They were all running all the time, making the cramped kitchen a sweltering inferno on the best of days and an inner ring of hell on the worst.

John, the sous-chef who managed the kitchen, had a forearm the size of my thigh, and when he gripped my hand to shake it, I could feel the calluses and scars that riddled his skin. He asked me to stand in a corner near the pastry station to observe, because the area had comparatively low traffic. John arranged a cutting board and knife there for me to use and showed me the proper way to dice an onion. "Grip the top with a fist, like this," he demonstrated, "That way if the knife slips, you don't cut yourself." I mimicked his actions. "Good," he said. "Now slice it crosswise like this, and then top to bottom." Perfect little squares of onion fell away from the core as he sliced. Something about taking something from nature and manipulating it into perfect geometric shapes struck me as beautiful. "Now you do it," John insisted, and lay a box of onions at my feet.

The Mexican guys did all the prep—peeling potatoes, rinsing salad greens, and laying out each ingredient for service in an organized fashion. They labored in silence until one of them would crack a joke in Spanish and all of them would erupt into laughter before settling back into a rhythm, slicing vegetables with surgical precision.

The restaurant owner's management style could best be described as benign neglect. I saw him only once after our first meeting, and so John and his motley crew of burly alcoholics were the ones running the show. They sauntered in late in the afternoon, after the prep had been completed, the sour odor of their hangover breath lingering faintly in the air behind them.

John and the others were like the performers who roll in just in time for the show after dedicated stagehands have set everything up for them. They often compared themselves to soldiers, but they struck me more as divas. If John walked in and the endive was not layered just so in the fridge, he would clench his fists around the container, shove it in the face of the nearest prep guy, and yell, "What the fuck is this?"

The role of the Irish guys—the sous-chef and line cooks—was to bang out dishes for guests. To apply the perfect amount of fire to the grilled langoustines that had been scrubbed and seasoned, to pan-fry the sole that had been delicately fileted for them to a caramel hue. Fire licked John's knuckles as he turned filet mignon over the flames, sweat beading above the bandanna on his forehead.

John would shout orders at the line cooks in an attempt to choreograph the timing of the food arriving at guest's tables. Getting different dishes to arrive at the same table hot and on time is like completing one of those Mensa puzzles about trains that leave varying stations at different times going different speeds and asking when they will converge in Milwaukee. If table four ordered steak and fish, here is what the math looks like. The steak, ordered medium-rare, will take four to seven minutes to cook while the fish will take three to five. The greens on the side of the fish will take two minutes to sear, while the carrots will be grilled for under a minute for the char. The mashed potatoes that go with the steak will take two minutes to heat (don't forget to stir occasionally!), unless you leave them over the flames too long while you were tending to the steak on the grill and the fish in a pan or the greens in another pan, in which case it will take six minutes because you will need to start over. All of these items must be delivered hot onto plates within a minute of each other because otherwise they start getting cold. They are seasoned one last time with a sprinkling of salt or a squeeze of lemon and garnished with herbs, then the plate is wiped clean around the edges and whisked away to the table.

This is just one order, for one table of two, and doesn't even include appetizers or dessert. Multiply this math problem by the 75 diners in the restaurant, and you start getting an idea about what an actual mind-fuck it is to execute this just right.

I would struggle to manage these logistics sober, but John consistently managed them drunk. The first round of drinks would arrive right before the first seating at 5:00 p.m., and the last one would arrive sometime around 1:00 a.m. The restaurant did not have a liquor license, so John would send a parade of food to the bar next door throughout the evening in exchange for a never-ending supply of booze.

After months of watching and a lifetime of home cooking, I was confident I could do some of the work on the line at least as well as some of my drunk comrades. John, not exactly the mentor of my dreams, did not seem to register my presence, so one night I decided to get pushy.

"John," I said, "it's really busy tonight. I'm confident I could handle the salad station. Let me jump in."

"Billy, where the fuck is that chicken for table two?" John barked, ignoring me completely.

"Still in hell, Chef," Billy shouted back, referring to the flames of the grill.

"Well, get that bitch out of there as soon as you can, okay?" John asked.

"Yes, Chef." Billy replied.

John turned back to me, wiping a bead of sweat from his forehead. "I dunno, hon—I think it's too crazy in here for you to step up tonight."

"We're one man down," I said, "and I know I can do this. If I were on salads, then Billy could focus on the meats and everything could get out more quickly. I've been practicing, and I've seen it done a thousand times. I can do this."

"Maybe tomorrow," John said, returning his attention to the grill. "Kevin—status update on the steak for table five? Everything else is being plated."

"One minute away, Chef," Kevin answered, lifting the meat with his tongs to gauge its progress.

"Crap," John responded. "Get your head out of your ass next time."

Each evening, the Mexicans and I prepped quietly in the corner while the Irish crew fired off expletives and assessed the state of various grilled meats. Night after night I would diligently chop my onions, watch the drama unfold, and wait for an invitation to step up to the plate. Night after night, the invitation never came. I was like a ghost on the sidelines, a grown-up version of that little girl at the soccer game waiting to play. Given how many vegetables I was chopping for free on the daily, I wanted a chance to really cook, to learn, to show what I could do. But if I was ever going to really play this game, it was clear I was going to have to join a different team.

6 | Working

Career, Job, or Hellscape?

"You have brains in your head. You have feet in your shoes. You can steer yourself any direction you choose."

—*Dr. Seuss*

When I was in third grade, my elementary school offered music lessons. I opted to learn the violin because my crush played the violin, and he sported a cute rattail haircut. If I could just sit behind him and his rattail every week, maybe, just maybe, it would improve my chances. Who knew what kind of magic would be made possible by the romantic sounds of the burgeoning string section?

Like everything else at my oversized public school, the music classes were conducted in very large groups. I missed the first few lessons and was too embarrassed to tell the teacher I didn't know what I was doing. So I showed up for the rest of the year and air-played the violin, so that I looked like I was playing but no sound came out. I hovered the bow just above the strings and followed the general direction of my classmates to give the appearance of playing. When their bows went up at a 45-degree angle, so did mine. When other kids' bows proceeded flat and slow along the strings, I leaned into the motion as though I had invented it. Up and down, back and forth, I became the Jimi Hendrix of the air violin, rocking out to nothing.

At the end of the school year, there was a mandatory test to determine each student's knowledge and assess their skill level for the following year. I was petrified. The teacher was going to find out that I had been faking it all year and would surely call home and expose me as a fraud to my parents. Given my parents' inconsolable disappointment at a recent B on a math quiz, I could not imagine what kind of reaction my feigned musical genius would elicit.

On the day of the test, I tried to fake being sick. I complained of a sore and scratchy throat, and body aches up and down my torso. My parents' work schedule did not have space for this kind of bullshit, and so when I didn't register a temperature, they kissed me on my forehead and sent me on my way. My palms were sweaty as I entered the lunchroom where the violin tests were set to begin. As I neared my seat, my throat began to constrict as my anxiety rose straight up from my belly and lodged there.

"Okay students," the music teacher called over the din. "Settle down, please!"

We all took our seats.

"We have a lot of tests to get through today, so we will be dividing you up into groups of five and you will be tested together."

Great. Now in addition to being mortified in front of the teacher, there would be four other students to witness my downfall.

So, this is how it ends, I thought.

As the other students began concentrating on their sheet music, I focused my attention on their body language. I gripped my bow in my fingers and hovered it ever so slightly above the strings at the same angles as my classmates. As I mimicked all their body movements, I could feel the sweat pooling just above my eyebrows, threatening to stream into my eyes. Up, down, left, right, I watched the students' bows intently and followed their movements, as I had for months.

When the song was over, I waited for the teacher to say something to me or to pull me aside. To ask me what on earth I had been doing all year, and why I didn't know how to play a single note. Instead, he casually dismissed us and let us know we'd receive a letter within the week about our placement for the following year.

A few days later, I arrived home and my father whisked me into his arms. "Congratulations, kiddo! You made it into the orchestra! We knew you must be a natural—we've never seen you practice but here you are making the orchestra after your first year of lessons. Your mom and I couldn't be prouder."

What. The. Actual. Fuck. Okay, I was in third grade. That sentence probably sounded more like: What. The. Actual. Fudge. How was I going to keep this charade going in the orchestra? Although my parents had lauded me as a child prodigy, I explained to them that I didn't want to play anymore. They skillfully applied a thick dose of Jewish guilt from all possible angles, but I wouldn't budge. I had just made it out of there by the skin of my teeth, and I didn't think my little heart could handle another episode like that test, nor the abject boredom of another year of faked lessons.

I used to think that there was little purpose to this story apart from its comedic value, but over time I have returned to it again and again for inspiration. The kernel I keep coming back to is that anything is possible when you put yourself out there, even when you don't know what the hell you're doing. I made it into orchestra without playing a note, just by having the gall to show up at the tryout. And while I can't recommend feigning skills for the purposes of impressing your crush, what I can recommend is having the chutzpah to show up for something that you want to learn and be a part of, even if you think you lack the skill to do it. I became a chef not by going to culinary school, but by asking to work in kitchens, even when I knew I would be the least knowledgeable person there. And unlike with the violin, I would raise my hand and ask about what I didn't know to keep improving. You can get a great education for free if you're willing to show up and be the dumbest one in the room for a while.

After months of apprenticing at the fancy restaurant, I was staring down the barrel of college graduation and felt like I was the only person without a clear path to follow when it ended. I watched my peers running around campus in suits, hopping purposefully from interview to interview, and found myself asking, "How did they even know these interviews existed?" Many were interviewing for lucrative positions as corporate consultants and investment bankers, and I didn't even know what those jobs were. My mom was a speech therapist and my dad an accountant, and the parents of my public-school friends had similarly straightforward middle-class jobs like teacher and nurse. I had never met a consultant or an investment banker—theirs was a world of high-earning esoteric work that felt a world away from the one I understood. I smiled and nodded knowingly when classmates named firms they were interviewing at, and I pretended that I just wasn't interested in those jobs even though I had no idea what they were or how to apply for them.

I wanted to move to New York City and convince someone to hire me to cook in their restaurant. Even though I hadn't exactly learned all that I had dreamed of in my brief tenure as an onion chopper over the past few months, the experience whetted my appetite to keep learning and growing as a chef. The sights and smells involved

> *You can get a great education for free if you're willing to show up and be the dumbest one in the room for a while.*

in being around food all day made me feel alive in a way that sitting in front of a computer did not, and all I knew was that I wanted to keep chasing that excited feeling in my gut. The problem was, I had no clue how to enter this unknown universe and this wasn't exactly the kind of role that the Princeton job center was prepared to help me with. Though it's hard to imagine in today's era of celebrity chefs, this was the time before food blogs even existed, let alone television networks dedicated to cooking. In the early aughts, streaming services didn't exist, and Marcus Samuelson was just a dude I could have a drink with after closing if I wandered into his restaurant.

I got a paid internship for the summer after graduation to bridge the gap and buy me some time to talk my way into kitchen work. Unfortunately for me, I soon learned that a kitchen interview is not like a normal job interview. You don't sit in a chair and answer questions or try to impress someone with your witty banter. A kitchen interview—called a stage—is where you provide free labor for eight hours while a chef watches you out of the corner of their eye. This practice is now no longer legal (was it ever?), but it was the only way to get hired.

After having put in only a few months at the New Jersey French restaurant run by alcoholics, my cooking displays were not particularly impressive. It would take me twice as long as other cooks to do whatever job I was given. I would invariably plate a dish incorrectly or not know how to slice carrots to the chef's specifications. I didn't understand half of the lingo floating about but was too embarrassed to ask anyone to clarify, so instead I would just make an ass of myself. For example, I did not know that the term "86" meant to run out of something, so when told by one chef to 86 arancini, I flew into a tizzy rummaging through every fridge looking for a giant tray of 86 nonexistent rice balls. The chef asked what I was doing, and when I told him, the entire kitchen erupted in laughter. I was like the Amelia Bedelia of kitchen help. They gave me the nickname Princeton for the rest of the shift to poke fun at my lack of genius.

After three months and dozens of failed interviews, my internship was about to run out. The organization I was working for offered me a full-time position, but I couldn't bear the thought of it. I began contemplating the exact level of shame involved in asking my parents to move back in with them. In the last week of my internship, I went on my worst restaurant interview ever, for a pastry position at an extremely high-profile American restaurant that was set to open in a few weeks on the Upper East Side of Manhattan. I had no experience in pastry other than enjoying making cookies with my dad growing up. I screwed up literally everything the chef asked me to do for him. I didn't weigh out some of the ingredients properly and in doing so botched a large batch of dough. I could not scoop ice cream in the proper form, so my plating resembled modern art executed by a five-year-old. I was, however, charming to talk to, and the pastry chef who had graduated with a degree in anthropology from NYU obviously saw something of himself in me, because he hired me in spite of it all. I couldn't believe it.

The job was an hour from the Brooklyn hovel I was living in, and I had to wake up at 4:30 in the morning to arrive at work on time at 6:00 a.m. I would pass the morning commute on the subway in a dream-state shared by the other unfortunate souls on the train at that hour. When I would finally get above ground it was still dark outside, and I would grab an egg sandwich from one of the ubiquitous street vendors and then go underground again into the windowless kitchen, where I would spend the next ten hours of my life.

This period of life was dark. And by dark, I mean literally. Between waking up at 4:30, my two-hour underground subway commute, and my ten-hour workdays and six-day workweek, I almost never saw the sun. It may have been summer in New York, but I felt like someone experiencing winter in Scandinavia—where each day I would emerge only to catch a glimmer of what seemed like a never-ending sunset between the skyscrapers. As a native Californian, I wish I could tell you that the deprivation from sunlight represented the bleakest part of this experience, but unfortunately, the darkness paled in comparison to the experience of actually working in the kitchen.

At the French restaurant in New Jersey, everyone was casual and fairly intoxicated, leaving me with a very specific view of what it might mean to be a chef. New York, however, was a different beast. This was a high-stakes opening of a multimillion-dollar restaurant with big-name chefs and even bigger-name investors. The restaurant was named after the building it was in—an architectural gem on the Upper East Side, and the reservation books were filled for weeks with some of New York's biggest players in finance and the arts. The interior of the space resembled a very tasteful honeycomb brought to life for the banker set. Coated in muted greys and greens, each table was punctuated by the warm glow of soft lighting that was inset to the wall and floorboards in a broad honeycomb pattern, inviting you to sit and make this your temporary hive. Fittingly, when filled with people, the space literally buzzed with the cacophony of its inhabitants—most likely from an acoustic plan that had taken a back seat to design.

While waiters would float in and out of this space, members of the kitchen staff were never allowed to be seen there. One day, I had to use the guest bathroom when the staff bathroom was being fixed, and the floor manager pulled me aside as he saw me standing there in my chef's whites. "What are you doing here?" he growled. When I pushed back, he asked me to join him back in the kitchen to discuss my transgression. "A magician never reveals their tricks. The food here—that is the magic. We never let our guests see behind the door—behind the curtain. You are destroying the experience—get back there immediately." I guess I would have to just hold it.

I had never really stopped to contemplate why we were held in a windowless room where none of the guests could see us. This was based on my naïve belief that we were cooking food, not making magic, and I would have to wrap my head around this new reality. The fucked-up thing was, if this was a magic show, we were the worst paid magicians on earth. The talent behind the show was making peanuts, while the ushers and cocktail waiters were making a small fortune. I was earning $10 an hour to make desserts, any one of which cost more than my hourly wage. Those bringing the desserts to the table, however, were earning $75 an hour in tips. This made little sense to me.

You might believe that because of this financial imbalance, the servers would be kind to the poor, underpaid souls making the food (nay, magic), but that was definitely not the case. Cold and demanding, the servers pushed the kitchen for the highest-quality food in the fastest time because their copious tips depended on it. In a way, I actually pitied them. I can only assume that their poor treatment of the kitchen staff represented a form of catharsis for the servers who were often berated by the demanding customer base paying top dollar for fine food and impeccable service. Out on the floor, the customer was in power, and behind the kitchen door, the servers were. So, like bullied kids, the servers would look to demean others to feel powerful or important because that was the only way they had ever seen it done.

This behavior was only further reinforced by the chefs, who all seemed to be trained in the same school of douchebaggery. My final day at this restaurant came when the abusive pastry chef that had so quickly taken to my talents witnessed two grave errors. For one, I had mistaken the sweet corn ice cream for the sweet cream ice cream and sent out a chocolate dessert with corn-flavored ice cream, leading to a disgusted and disgruntled guest. The chef accused me of sabotage. Later that day, I plated a scoop of ice cream at a 15-degree angle on the plate instead of 45 degrees as instructed. "Where the fuck do you think you are?!" he screamed, "Friendly's?!"

I decided at that moment that I was not sure what I was doing in this underground dungeon presided over by this aggressive dragon of a pastry chef. I went home and started looking for a new job. Thankfully, working at the fancy restaurant was like dating Beyoncé—now that I had this rare experience on my résumé, I was a lot more desirable in the restaurant market.

7 | Detours

The Hallmark of a Worthwhile Career or Memorable Vacation

"My mother always used to say: The older you get, the better you get, unless you're a banana."

—*Rose (Betty White) on* The Golden Girls

My first interview after leaving the fancy restaurant was at a hip neighborhood spot in a run-down neighborhood in Brooklyn that had yet to be gentrified, but in ensuing years would become unrecognizable. Housed in a brick building directly beneath the Manhattan Bridge, the entire restaurant shook every time the subway rumbled overhead. The street leading up to the restaurant had eroded away to uncover the underlying cobblestones, which peeked out every few feet in the deeply pocketed road.

I interviewed with the head chef, a butch lesbian who never asked me to display any of my cooking skills but just asked for war stories from my current job. She hired me—whether because my stories amused her, she thought I was cute, or she found my résumé impressive, I will never know. Too much of a coward to tell my old boss that he was the real reason I was leaving, I lied and told him I was experiencing family problems and needed to leave New York. I guess I was banking on the fact that he would never go to Brooklyn to eat and see me cooking somewhere else. At the time, Brooklyn was still not cool and thus it was a pretty safe bet.

Life at the Brooklyn restaurant—let's call it Ubercool—was a complete 180 from my job on the Upper East Side. I wore jeans, a T-shirt, and an apron instead of chef's whites. Instead of cooking in an underground dungeon, the kitchen was open so the cooks could see the entire dining room and speak with the guests. Instead of being owned by investors in suits, Ubercool was owned by three lesbians who had lived in the neighborhood for years in various permutations of dating and living with each other. One of the women managed the bar, one the kitchen, and one the floor, and they were each an archetype of the area they managed. The bar manager was a wild, tattooed blond who would dance on the bar on busy nights. The floor manager was a warm and bubbly presence with frizzy hair who could never remember basic operational details but had memorized the names and orders of hundreds of regulars whom she greeted with a hug. The chef was a moody but brilliant creative type who rode a motorcycle to work and used her cooking talents to seduce and bang women who were always squarely out of her league. Their incestuous trifecta represented the best and worst of the restaurant world, and seemed to strike a perfect balance that has lasted to this day—they are still open as of this writing more than 20 years later.

Working at Ubercool, I began learning all the things about food and cooking I had hoped for when I started down this windy path. I learned how to grind homemade sausage so that it has just the right ratio of fat to meat, and how to season it so that the flavors pop on the first bite. I was shown how to properly rinse and store salad greens so that the dish would feel alive on the plate when it arrived before a guest. The staff was welcoming, and we would commune every morning over a shared meal of stewed beans, rice, and New Mexico hatch chiles that the chef imported from her home state. The guests were warm, mostly regulars, and the owners threw a giant neighborhood Thanksgiving potluck where hundreds of people showed up to break bread. There was a bluegrass brunch every Sunday, where I would tap my feet to the twang of the banjo as I plated heaps of homey fare to nurse guests' hangovers from the weekend's debauchery.

Cooking in a restaurant like Ubercool is simultaneously dulling and invigorating. I arrived at work to the same prep list every day—chopping and sautéing onions and peppers, rinsing and prepping salad greens, and making sure the entire line was stocked up for a busy lunch service. I would then spend a few hours cooking dishes like linguine with homemade sausage for customers, where my crude multitasking skills were tested in rapid-fire succession. Honestly, I was not great at timing dishes to come out at the same time, and my body's response to the stress was to curl up my toes so tightly I would cause myself to get leg cramps.

After all the hours on my feet and the crummy paycheck that barely paid the rent of my Brooklyn hovel, there were a few glorious moments each day where it all seemed worth it. When I would lean over a pot of a new dish and inhale the aroma of a spice I had never smelled. When a guest would lean over the counter into the kitchen and tell me how the meal I cooked for them brightened their day. When I would leave work, my legs shaking and exhausted, and sit in the park across the way nursing a warm drink and breathing in the New York skyline.

I lived in a railroad apartment in Brooklyn with two roommates. My room had no access to natural light, with a single window aimed at an air shaft. The room was so small that I couldn't fit a desk in it, so I purchased a flip-up desk from Ikea and proudly installed it myself. I didn't realize you need to anchor it to studs, so two days later my pièce de résistance ripped out the larger part of my wall.

I made $10 an hour, so working full time was pulling in $1,600/month and came with no health benefits or paid time off. So even if I worked 40 hours a week and never got sick or took any vacation, I was still earning less than $20,000 a year and attempting to live in New York City. I spent more than 50 percent of my income on rent and utilities and couldn't afford to eat at any of the restaurants I worked in.

One day, I went to visit my friend Glenn from Princeton. He had taken one of those investment banking jobs that I still didn't understand and was too embarrassed to ask about. Glenn made more than six times my annual salary, and when I entered his apartment, it felt like a spa. There was soft lighting and a lightly scented lemongrass candle burning gently in the bathroom. Glenn had no roommates, and floor-to-ceiling windows that overlooked the glittering Manhattan skyline. He served me a vodka tonic on ice, and as I took in the view from his temperature-controlled high rise, I began dreading returning to my sweltering hovel on this steamy summer night.

I loved the buzz of restaurants, and living my days steeped in the smells and tastes of steaks charred by fire and freshly plucked herbs. But the fact that I couldn't see a path to the kind of life that Glenn had just one year out of college even after a lifetime of cooking was disturbing to me. Even if I worked my ass off, it was hard to see how I would ever amass any savings, let alone the amount necessary to start my own place. To attract investors, most chefs need to put in about a decade of time in kitchens, which was a lot of time to spend living below the poverty line. Even the owners at Uber-cool were still renting their own apartments, unable to afford to buy their own place.

The day I realized I had to leave Ubercool was actually one of my favorite days there—the holiday party. The owners did not tell us what we were going to do—just that they were closing the restaurant for the night and that we should meet there at 7 p.m. After plying their heavily queer, heavily tattooed and pierced staff with alcohol and a variety of catered mezze, they ushered us outside, where a psychedelic school bus awaited to take us to a mystery destination. The owners proceeded to pass around mushrooms—not of the culinary variety—while the bar manager danced provocatively on a stripper pole in the middle of the multicolored bus.

After an extremely long ride featuring disco lights and thumping old-school party music, we arrived at a bowling alley which the owners had rented out completely for the party. If you are living in Wisconsin, this might not seem that out of the ordinary, but in New York City space is such an expensive commodity that finding and renting an entire bowling alley for a party is an act of extreme generosity. Awash in a haze of drugs and alcohol, everyone danced along the lanes, hugged, and teased each other as they attempted to corral the balls into the correct lanes. The sound of pins crashed in the background as people groped each other and the backs of chairs in an attempt to find stability.

As the group formed a conga line through the aisles of the vacant bowling alley, I looked around with a sinking feeling in the pit of my stomach despite the elation that surrounded me. I wasn't sure if this was where I imagined my life headed. I looked at my bosses, completely high and hitting mercilessly on my date for the evening, and asked myself if this was really what I aimed to become. Drenched in the sensuality that a life of food brings out, everything around me felt infused with electricity—exciting but completely unstable. The punishing hours, the low pay, the eccentric personalities—it had all the makings of a great party, but not the foundation of a stable life the morning after. I had a vision of the years ahead of me that looked a lot like this one and wondered what the fuck I was doing at an abandoned bowling alley in the nether reaches of Brooklyn, surrounded by hallucinating lesbians.

I woke up the following morning, dusted the sleep from my eyes, and told myself I was going to make a grown-up decision about my career. No more windowless apartments or drug-addled holiday parties. The only problem: food was all I had ever really wanted to do. So I did what smart people with no direction have been doing for generations: I decided to apply to law school.

Many people have asked me why I decided to go to law school in the first place, given my passion for restaurants. I did it partly because of how demoralizing it was to be broke in one of the most expensive cities in the world. I also did it because of extreme pressure from my well-meaning Jewish parents. But mostly, I didn't

The punishing hours, the low pay, the eccentric personalities—it had all the makings of a great party, but not the foundation of a stable life the morning after.

have a model for what success that didn't go in a straight line looked like. How do you become a restaurant owner, instead of just someone working in one? No one tells you how to do things like that.

School trains you for a life of straight lines from point A to point B. The basic rules are this. Someone in power (a teacher) tells you what you need to do to succeed. The more you do exactly what they say, the better you'll do. In school, we're given a syllabus telling us what we will learn, a reading list telling us what to read, study guides telling us what we need to know, and tests to figure out just how well we've conformed to learning what someone else thought we should know in just the way they want us to know it.

I played by all the rules growing up. I listened in school, raised my hand, got A's. Unless you were lucky enough to go to some kind of alternative hippie school where they called teachers by their first names and doled out marijuana at recess, you also likely attended a school that trained you exquisitely for a life of straight lines. The more you listen to authority and don't veer from the prescribed course set for you, the more positive reinforcement you'll receive. It comes in the form of grades, accolades, awards, approval, and admission to even more schools that do the same thing.

So we do this for 18 years (22 if you go to college, even longer if you go to grad school!). When we're finished, we start looking for things that mirror this system we feel so incredibly used to. We look for someone else to tell us how to be successful, because we've been trained to do this. We're good at this! It's why the vast majority of people will apply for jobs where they perform a list of tasks that someone else has set out for them, just like a teacher for a student. We undergo extensive training doing what an authority figure tells us we must do to be successful. This is the system we've been taught to work within. It looks exactly like school, except instead of grades we get money—a grown-up form of approval.

I went to law school because I had reached the outer limits of my comfort zone navigating a curvy path. There was no special system designed to take me where I wanted to go. For all my education, I couldn't figure out how to move from making minimum wage to having a sustainable career in food. And having only ever done what other people had asked of me, I lacked the self-confidence to imagine something different. When you've spent your entire existence walking as narrowly as possible on the path that teachers, parents, and school have forged for you, it is hard to make your own way. So I bailed. I got back on a path that felt comfortable, even if I knew in my bones it wasn't right for me.

I won't bore you with the details, but I spent five years on the fruitless detour that was my life as a lawyer, culminating in the day I was let go and resolved to rededicate myself to restaurants and food. To mark the occasion, I decided to get an asparagus tattoo. I had wanted an asparagus tattoo for as long as I could remember, but everyone in my life placed the idea somewhere between

When you've spent your entire existence walking as narrowly as possible on the path that teachers, parents, and school have forged for you, it is hard to make your own way.

misguided and moronic. However, I have found that sometimes, if you want something for long enough, you will stop caring about what other people think and do it anyway.

The first time I read about asparagus, I was mesmerized by the story of its life. Before the first edible spear ever appears, asparagus plants spend two years constructing an intricate network of roots beneath the ground. When it is time for the spears to emerge, they do so in places that cannot be predicted or controlled. An asparagus field will look like a disparate array of stalks, but actually they are all connected beneath the surface by a wild array of roots.

Asparagus is the first sign of spring, of renewal and new growth. I fell in love with its life story because it was such a beautiful metaphor for how we all live our lives—reaching blindly beneath the surface in so many directions, never knowing where exactly we will grow up next but having all of our experiences merged beneath the surface in an intricate, jumbled, but unified pattern uniquely our own. When we are ready, we reach for the sun and emerge—standing in one spot, but connected fundamentally to so many others.

As I lay back in the tattoo artist's chair, I felt as though she were slicing my skin for the better part of two hours, until finally, the slices emerged as thin black lines that constructed the outline of my favorite plant. What she had drawn was not an asparagus spear, but rather the wild, spiky branches of a mature asparagus plant. Very few people other than asparagus farmers have any clue what an asparagus plant actually looks like, but it resembles a dense green, wispy fern.

The leaves of the plant on my arm looked like softer versions of pine needles, and the thin branch that held them together was dotted with bulbs and tiny bell-shaped flowers. I thought it was beautiful, and larger than I had anticipated. The artist wiped me down, then bandaged my raw pink flesh in some kind of medical-grade coating, and then, very unceremoniously, covered it in Saran wrap. I emerged from the studio with my arm looking like a poorly packaged burrito.

All of our experiences, even the ones we regret as an abject waste of time, are still forming little interconnected nodes beneath the ground, ready to spring toward the sky when the time is right.

Long since healed, my tattoo reminds me that even after we decide to walk down a more straight-lined career path, the arc of life is never so clean. And all of our experiences, even the ones we regret as an abject waste of time, are still forming little interconnected nodes beneath the ground, ready to spring toward the sky when the time is right.

8 | Startup

The First Wobbly Steps of a Baby Business

"The secret to getting ahead is getting started."

—*Agatha Christie*

Looming large over my parents' front yard is a spectacular Meyer lemon tree. Meyer lemons are a touch sweeter than the Lisbon lemons found in supermarkets, and a ton juicier. Their skin is thin, and when you squeeze them the tart, tangy juice flows out like water from a spigot. As a ten-year-old confronted by a bounty of juicy lemons right in my front yard, I did what any young, entrepreneurial kid would do, and made a lemonade stand. I would wake up early on Sunday mornings, and after filling my head with cartoons I'd run outside to pluck a few low-hanging fruits, squeeze them between my hands into a large pitcher, and dump in generous amounts of sugar and a few splashes of water. I then poured ice out of the freezer into my dad's bar bucket so the ice wouldn't dilute the thick lemonade, and hauled my pitcher outside with a handful of flimsy Dixie cups. I charged 25 cents a cup, and proudly earned an average of $3.50 a day to support my weekly Butterfinger habit at the local liquor store.

I really thought I was crushing it at life until my younger brother, Stephen, decided to operate his own lemonade business. Stephen was too little to make homemade lemonade, so he whipped up a batch of Country Time powdered pink lemonade instead. He branded his business "Pick Your Price" lemonade, and offered customers the chance to drink their lemonade first and then decide what it was worth second. Confronted with a gap-toothed five-year-old asking how much they thought his product was worth, customers were generous. Most left at least a dollar— four times what I was charging—but many left more. Much more. One guy on a motorcycle stopped by and dropped Stephen a $20. This was the '80s, folks. That is the equivalent of $70 today.

With a distinctly subpar product, Stephen made more in one day than I made all year. What I learned: pricing is everything.

Having departed my legal career, I was just starting to work on my mac and cheese business when I first heard about an event called the Underground Market. It was like a secretive underground disco, but instead of edgy bands, it featured all kinds of illegal food vendors. This was 2010 and with America deep in a recession, many people who were out of work started cooking and selling food out of their home kitchens.

The Underground Market was housed in a large warehouse space with a DJ spinning music from a platform overhead. The application process consisted of tracking down the guy who put together the event and asking to participate. If accepted, vendors were assigned a small square of space from which to sell and set up stands with makeshift posters, like at a science fair.

There was a $5 cover charge, and bouncers at the front door managed a line that snaked three blocks long to get in. In a time where every day brought bleak news about a foreclosure crisis and largescale layoffs, the public was hungry for something that made them feel like there was still vibrancy and hope to be enjoyed. The energy in the line was palpable.

I arrived at the market simultaneously lifted off the ground by adrenaline and shoved back down by exhaustion. My prep had begun the week before, as I began tracking down enough ingredients to feed people the hundreds of pounds of macaroni and cheese I was going to be cooking. I had never made this much before, and pulling this off was a juggling act between sourcing, storage, and prep.

I rode my bicycle around Oakland, stopping at every single grocery store to buy them out of my favorite kinds of dried pasta and cheese. The pasta was a chubby, rounded, oversized elbow noodle made by a popular pasta brand, but most stores only stocked a few boxes of it. I got one store to order an entire case of it, but everywhere else would just sell me whatever they had on hand. I would wind my way back to my apartment slowly through tree-lined streets of Craftsman homes, blaring Cat Power through my headphones, and making a note of which places carried the most for future reference. I would dump the boxes on my living room floor, stacking them until I had amassed so many that they blocked the entrance to the room altogether, and then head out again looking for more. The quest for cheese was a similar endeavor, except that my refrigerator became a dedicated cheddar holding cell.

The day before the event I started cooking right after my morning coffee at 7 a.m. I thought it might take me eight to ten hours—instead it took eighteen. The pasta took the longest to cook, and it required a Herculean effort to transfer pounds of cooked noodles into the gigantic buckets I had purchased from the restaurant supply store. Slowly, the boxes of dried elbow pasta in my living room were replaced with buckets upon buckets of cooked al dente pasta, stacked atop each other like restaurant-grade Lincoln logs.

I started grating the cheese by pressing it through the grating attachment of my Cuisinart. It turns out these machines were not meant to process industrial-grade amounts of cheese, and soon the acrid smoke of the equipment's burning motor filled my apartment. I ran out to the store to buy a grating attachment for my stand mixer, but it was comically inefficient at the task. I ended up grating the remaining 20 pounds by hand over a box grater, and sliced two fingers to shreds in the process.

With my Band-Aid-riddled fingertips, I whisked together gallons upon gallons of bechamel cream sauce. This is one of the so-called French mother sauces, the kind of thing people go to culinary school to learn how to make properly. I did not go to culinary school, and I would routinely fuck it up. The process goes something like this—you begin by toasting flour in butter, which is a deeply temperamental step. If you don't cook the flour enough, your sauce will taste chalky because you have uncooked flour swirling about, but if you cook the flour too much, your sauce will taste nutty at best and like Starbucks coffee at worst (sorry Starbucks fans). Once the flour is cooked just right, you slowly pour in hot milk and whisk like your life depends on it. Whisk too slowly, and the sauce seizes up and produces lumpy chunks of flour-riddled sauce that taste like a bland, chewy dumpling. If whisked just perfectly, the cooked flour thickens the milk, and yields a silky, creamy base to which you can later add your cheese.

Timing the cooking of the flour, the whisking of the milk, the draining of the pasta, and the grating of the cheese just right was nearly impossible, and I was losing an unacceptable amount of product to being burned or overcooked. My tiny apartment kitchen filled with steam no matter how many windows I opened, and it was like cooking in the middle of a Russian spa. Sweat dripped out of my pores as I blared MGMT's latest album and whirled around my kitchen. As the hours ticked by in my homemade sauna, my energy evolved from manic to panic. How many boxes left? How much time per box to cook? Why can't I feel my right arm anymore? Will I ever sleep again?

Spent, I cooked my last box of pasta at one o'clock in the morning. I wish I could tell you I had proper storage for all of this food, but I stored all the pasta and grated cheese in a giant tower in my living room, while the cream sauce lived in the fridge. I fell into bed and prayed to whoever was up there that the food would not rot by the following day.

The next day I transferred the mountain of food from my living room into my battered sedan. Only a fraction of it fit in the car with me, so I had to make three trips across the Bay Bridge to San Francisco and back. When I arrived at the market to unload, other vendors were undergoing a similar process of lugging awkward containers out of vans, trucks, and even a motorcycle. The cavernous space started to fill with fold-out tables and colorful signs and was buzzing with frenetic energy.

As the contours of the market began to take shape, I took a pause in my own setup to wander the floor and take it all in. The room was bursting with a wide range of hopefuls hawking foods as distinctive as their personalities. An exuberant former tech bro preached about his freshly squeezed sugarcane juice, a lesbian couple offered pies in flavors ranging from classic apple to ube-pecan, a man with a possibly fake Jamaican accent sold intensely smoky jerk chicken, and a waif-like woman made fruit sorbets so intense she sold them by the thimbleful.

The level of care and detail that people took in carefully constructing their booths and tending to their food gave me goosebumps. There was something downright magical about being in a room filled with people who had spent their night in roughly the same kind of hell that I had in order to share something of themselves with hundreds of strangers. For most of us, this was the first time we would be sharing our food with the public, and there was a sense of camaraderie as we helped each other at the loading dock or gave the thumbs up as someone hoisted their sign into the air.

A ragtag bunch of friends and family rolled in to help me set up my booth and staff it for the evening. We were making two kinds of mac and cheese: a classic cheddar mac, and so-called trailer mac, which was a classic with hot dogs and topped with potato chips. We set up an assembly line of sorts—with me and a friend cooking over induction burners in the back— stirring the pasta with the cream sauce and melting the cheese down into it to gooey perfection. One person would be taking money at the front, and the other would dish up the mac and hand it to customers.

Our sign was handmade and hung on the wall behind us, while our table was destabilized by a wobbly leg. We all wore matching shirts and aprons to give the appearance of professionalism, but we still looked like slackers at the science fair compared to how professional some of the vendors' signage and setup was. One woman had created an entire cardboard storefront to resemble a fairytale house, and she would sell slices of pie by dipping her head in and out of a mock kitchen window. Our stand was neither adorable nor impressive like hers, but I knew that our mac and cheese was going to be first-rate, and I hoped that would be enough.

After my weeklong pasta raids of every grocery store in Oakland and my night of fever dream cooking, I was ready to feed hundreds of people. I had the ingredients ready to be fired up, my janky table ready to do business, and a legion of friends at the ready to stir mac and cheese until their arms gave out. But what if, after all that fuss, no one wanted to buy what I was selling? What if I had left my stable job to start a business making something that no one really wanted? It felt like less of a referendum on my mac and cheese and more like a referendum on my life choices. My crippling insecurity led me to price my product so low it bordered on ridiculous—my hope was that no one would think twice about buying it, and I could avoid confronting my own existential dread for the evening. It was $2 for a heaping bowl.

The lights in the room were dimmed and the disco ball began to twirl, cascading a confetti of light around the cavernous space. The DJ began spinning a bass-filled beat, and the doors were opened for customers to start shuffling in.

The first people in the door moved quickly, trying to take everything in and scoop up food before the hordes behind them made it into the room. We had our first customer within minutes. The system we developed for the market would end up being the same one we would use at the restaurant a year later, and forever after. At most restaurants (or family picnics), mac and cheese is usually a side dish, or an afterthought. It will sit in a big tray or warmer, the noodles growing soggier by the second, the cheese sauce getting dried out and grainy. For mac and cheese to really get the spotlight, it needs to be fresh. It is at its most creamy, tangy, and alive when it is piping hot and fresh from the stovetop, so we cooked our mac to order. We would blend together the al dente pasta, cream sauce, and cheese over induction burners until they melted together and became one. We would then dish up the batch into a dozen little bowls, and hand it out to customers who had just paid.

I watched as our first customer—a 20-something Asian woman dolled up for a night on the town, dug into her bowl. A smile spread across her face as the cheese pulled up from her fork as she hoisted a noodle out of the cream sauce. When she put the pasta in her mouth, she closed her eyes for a second, and let a delighted "Mmm" escape her closed lips. I exhaled—she got it. Something inside me knew it was going to be okay.

I quickly flipped back to the line forming in front of our booth. Everything at the market had been priced and portioned to be a main dish—a full slice of pie, an entire sandwich, a bowl of curry—all between $8 and $10. I can't say that my intense fear of failure has served me many times in my life, but my strategy (if it can be called that) of grossly underpricing my food so that maybe people would want it made our booth the breakout star of the night. People might question if they want to invest $10 on an entire sandwich at an event where they want to try a lot of food, but no one will question spending $2 on a bowl of mac and cheese.

Our line snaked around the room, and we could not cook mac and cheese fast enough to keep up with the enthusiastic hordes of people waiting for it. At the front table, my friend was taking rapid-fire orders and counting cash, then sending folks along to pick up their piping bowl of mac from the line of friends aggressively stirring pots of mac to perfection. Most people have only ever cooked mac and cheese from a box, if at all, and seeing a fresh batch get whipped up in front of them brought forth actual squeals of delight. People were snapping pictures and videos and their enthusiasm was practically boiling over by the time they were handed their overflowing bowl of mac.

We ran out of food in an hour and a half, and there wasn't a soul in that room not carrying a bowl of our mac. We served 900 people. It was on.

9 | Luck

So Important It's Unsettling

"Unexpected kindness is the most powerful, least costly, and most underrated agent of human change. Kindness that catches us by surprise brings out the best in our natures."

—*Bob Kerrey*

Starting a business is a little bit like planning a vacation, except if you stripped the trip of all the things that made it relaxing. You might have a business plan—an itinerary—but those are just the guideposts of where you hope to go. What you actually do is often defined by the random encounters you have along the way, the ones you cannot possibly plan. The person who helps (or doesn't) when you're lost. A chance meeting that changes your perspective. As someone who likes to feel in control of their destiny, I have always found it a little bit frightening that so much of my own trajectory has depended on the kindness of strangers. This is the story of two of the very best.

When I was 23, I took a solo trip to Japan. After arriving in Osaka, my adrenaline-addled body was overcome by the blinking neon signs that littered the landscape as harried men in crisp suits rushed by. This was a pre-smartphone era and I had not booked a hotel, so my plan was to wander the streets with my oversize backpack until I found a place to stay.

I looked like a strung-out hippie with floppy pants reminiscent of MC Hammer, a faded henna tattoo around my ankle, and my dirty-blond hair in a rat's nest of a top bun. I scoured the streets of Osaka for hours but was waved away everywhere I went. I couldn't tell if I was being denied service because of my haggard appearance, or because they were legitimately full, but as night fell, the electrical pulse of panic set in. I stood in the middle of the sidewalk staring blankly at my guidebook and suppressing my tears, when an elderly woman tapped me on the shoulder.

"Hello," she said. "Are you looking for a hotel?"

"Oh," I said, "thanks for asking. I'm not looking for one in particular, but I've been wandering for hours and can't find any hotel with a free room."

"Yes," the woman said, "there is a big conference right now, so most hotels are full. Do you want to come to my apartment and I can call some for you? This way you don't have to walk around with your big bag."

I looked her up and down. She must have been about 70 years old, with a sturdy build and tidy gray hair. Her outfit was pressed, pristine. I did a gut-check. She felt safe.

"My name is Tamae," she offered. "I like to travel, and many people have helped me in other countries. Let me help you."

"Thank you," I said, relieved, and followed her down the street.

Tamae led me into her apartment, a simple, clean space arranged in the traditional Japanese style with tatami floors and translucent shoji screens separating the rooms. She offered me green tea, which I happily accepted, and sat next to me on the couch as she dialed hotel after hotel, inquiring about rooms. After trying about 15 places, she turned to me and offered, "I think everywhere is full. Do you want to stay here?" I said yes.

I wrote my parents from an internet cafe to relate my good fortune. The reply from my father, verbatim:

Erin:

> I doubt that you are still up and about but if you are I would get out of that apartment and check into a hotel pronto. Your situation is just too good to be true. The technique you described is a classic pickup for white slavery. Be careful of accepting drinks etc. from the woman. You ought to get out of there as soon as you can, like this minute. Please reply as soon as possible.

I completely ignored my father's paranoid advice and ended up staying with Tamae for two nights, during which the most dangerous thing to befall me was a lunchtime run-in with *natto*, a local delicacy of fermented soybeans that taste like smelly cheese (I couldn't stomach them). Tamae never let me pay her for anything, and she even took me out to dinner with her friends, a small cadre of warm, chatty women who mixed up their Japanese with English, to make me feel included. The only thing she asked for in return was when I returned to America, to send her those floss sticks with the plastic prongs. Apparently they don't have them in Japan, and she thought they were superior to all Japanese dental hygiene products. I sent her three giant boxes of them.

I had meticulously planned my trip to Japan but to this day I don't remember the details of the temples I visited or the names of the hotels I stayed at. What sticks with me are the nights at Tamae's apartment and the rich flavor of the smoky yakitori skewers I shared with her and her friends. Tamae and I remained pen pals for years, and her generosity toward a complete stranger always stuck with me.

Tamae's hospitality is one of the things I reach for when I think of what the word means. She is one of a few guardian angels I've been lucky enough to have. The person who helped me secure Homeroom's location was the other.

At the time, my burgeoning business was crushing it at mobile events, but I didn't want to be cooking macaroni and cheese illegally out of my apartment for the rest of my life. I named the business Homeroom for its double meaning: a nostalgic nod to the class in school that serves no real purpose other than reconnecting with friends, as well as a reference to a room in one's home. I wanted Homeroom to be a place that felt as comfortable, fun, and inviting as a cozy dinner party. The only problem: Homeroom needed a home.

I had no idea how commercial real estate worked, so I did what any clueless aspiring restaurateur would do—I wandered the streets looking for FOR LEASE signs, jotted down their numbers, and hoped that someone would return my phone calls. I didn't realize that most reputable businesspeople do this work through brokers—sort of like looking for a house—so I sounded like a total clown calling on my own behalf. It gave me away as a rookie, which, considering how fickle restaurants are as a business, no reputable broker was interested in engaging with. I would get one phone call back for every 20 or so I made. Of those, a tiny fraction still wanted to speak with me after hearing that I was going to open a mac and cheese restaurant.

This made little sense to me, because Oakland was littered with empty storefronts. It was years into America's mortgage crisis, where both residential and commercial real estate markets had cratered, and entire blocks of Oakland storefronts stood vacant and decaying. But because commercial real estate thrives on long, lucrative leases, owners would rather have their storefront sit empty than take a bad bet on a girl with an eccentric restaurant idea.

I thought that renting a commercial space would be akin to renting an apartment, but it's more like renting a campsite and then having to build your own apartment on the land, then leaving it there for the owner when your lease is up. I don't know who designed this feudal system, but commercial spaces are generally rented as what's called a "vanilla shell" (a yummy name for a yucky concept). That means what you are renting is a slab of concrete with no gas, plumbing, toilets, sinks, closets, walls, electricity, or anything else you might need to do a damn thing in there other than have a rousing game of wall-ball. You have to run all those lines yourself, buy your own fixtures, put up your own walls, along with everything else you might need for your own business. If you're successful, when your lease is up you will leave all these expensive improvements in there so that the landlord can charge the next tenant more for all these things *you* paid for. And if you fail, the shortest lease is generally about five years long, so you're really locked into your extravagantly expensive failure. Awesome.

I had spent months negotiating a lease on a space, only to have the landlord double the rent on the day of signing, so I walked away from the deal. I spent the next week feeling sorry for myself, eating vast amounts of Chunky Monkey on my couch, and binge-watching *Sex and the City*. I decided to take one more stab at finding a location, and this time I would only look off the beaten path of the established neighborhoods I had been looking in. I rode my bike all over the city, searching for anything that looked promising. One day, on my ride home, I passed a FOR LEASE sign in the window of a new-looking building I had never noticed before. It was on a major street, just a few blocks from public transit, and across the street from a plumbing supply store with the largest window display of toilets I had ever seen. I called the number immediately.

That night, I went back to do a customer count. This is where you sit on the sidewalk and count the foot traffic to get a sense of how many potential customers would walk by on an average evening. Since this was not one of the buzzy areas I had been looking at, I wanted to have a sense of the nightlife.

When I arrived, the street was eerily desolate, without even streetlights to brighten the sidewalk. There were no other businesses open for a few blocks in either direction, and the only sounds were cars whizzing by on their way to other, more interesting places. The customer count proved an easy exercise, because no one was walking by. Eventually two people did, greeting each other on the adjacent corner, and engaging in what appeared to be a drug deal before walking briskly away from each other.

The next day a chipper man returned my call about the space. Not surprisingly, it was still available, and had sat vacant for the last three years. The price was more expensive than others I had been considering, and this building was in a far riskier bet of a neighborhood. Other spots I had looked at were surrounded by busy offices and other restaurants, cafes, bars, and nightlife. This one sat alone on an empty street blocks from anything else that was even open, let alone desirable. I decided to sit down with the owner to negotiate.

The owner was a man named Mark, who, like most commercial landlords, appeared to own vast swaths of the neighborhood. He was an affable architect whose office was a few doors down from the space we were negotiating, and he greeted me warmly when I walked in the door.

"Welcome," he said. "Please take a seat. Can I grab you some coffee?"

"No," I said, jittery already, "I'm extremely caffeinated, but appreciate the offer."

He laughed. "Okay, then," he remarked, "I read through your business plan and I think you'd make a great addition to the neighborhood. Exactly what we need around here."

"Thanks," I said. "Most people think the idea is a little kooky, so I'm glad you like it."

"Any chance you might add a sandwich to the menu?" he asked. "I could really use a spot to grab a good sandwich around here."

"Great idea," I said, "I'll think about it." There was no way in hell I was diluting my idea with sandwiches, but people were giving me unsolicited business advice all the time and I had learned it was more important to make them feel good than to tell them the truth.

"Should we get down to business?" Mark asked.

"Let's do it." I countered.

"I am proposing fairly standard terms," Mark said. "I'm not sure if you had a chance to review them."

"I have," I said, "and I don't have any issues, except for the price."

"Well, that's sort of an important one," he chuckled.

"I don't think what you're asking is unreasonable," I said. "The truth is, the space is bigger than others I looked at, and I simply can't afford it."

"It's 1100 square feet," said Mark. "That's pretty small."

"So is my budget," I joked.

He laughed.

"Seriously though," I continued, "I think we could bring a lot to the neighborhood. Homeroom already has a dedicated following, and I will personally put my heart and soul into making this restaurant a beautiful space that draws people in."

"So how much of a haircut are you wanting me to take?" Mark asked.

"I want to pay half of what you're quoting."

"Half?!" Mark choked on his coffee.

"Yes, half," I said. "I know it's not fair, it's just what I have. And even if I did have more money, I wouldn't take a bet on a risky neighborhood."

"But that's so much less than asking," said Mark.

"I realize that you'll probably lose money on this deal, but this neighborhood is absolutely dead at night and there's a reason this building has been vacant for three years. I know you own like half the buildings in this neighborhood, and Homeroom is the spark that this street needs. I'm asking you to take a risk on me, but I will be risking my life savings to take a bet on you, too. My hope is that Homeroom gives the whole neighborhood a much-needed lift, and brings the value of your other properties up with it. And I'll throw in a lifetime of free mac and cheese for you and your family," I added.

Mark smiled. "Now that is compelling." He sat for a moment, fidgeting with his pencil and staring down at the expanse of table between us.

"Look," he said, "I'm not thrilled about this, but I have a good feeling about you. I genuinely want this neighborhood to have more life in it, and it needs to start somewhere. I'm willing to try this, but please don't let me down."

Tiny bombs of nervous energy exploded in the pit of my stomach.

"I won't!" I exclaimed, "You will not regret this—I promise!"

They say that success is one part skill and one part dumb luck. I was lucky to have someone as generous as Mark on the other side of that negotiation table. However, a former, less desperate version of myself would have been too embarrassed to ask for a 50 percent reduction in the price of a candy bar, let alone a piece of real estate. I learned that you can't get what you don't ask for, and by framing a short-term loss as a long-term gain, my skill helped tilt the scales. Finding a path toward joint success is the joy beneath any good business deal. And I made good on my promise—within five years, the street was buzzing with activity and all of Mark's vacant real estate on the street was rented.

10 | Perseverance

Why Grit Matters
More Than Wit

"Champions aren't made in gyms, champions are made from something they have deep inside them—a desire, a dream, a vision. They have to have last-minute stamina, they have to be a little faster, they have to have the skill and the will. But the will must be stronger than the skill."

—*Muhammad Ali*

Around the age of nine, I decided that I really wanted a pet. I don't recall if my desire for something cuddly to take care of was brought on as an antidote to early teenage angst or just by a really good episode of *Alvin and the Chipmunks,* but I was dying for a dog, cat, hamster...anything really.

I prepared a list of reasons for my parents as to why I would be particularly suited to be a pet parent, and argued my case over dinner one night. As working parents of three who liked to keep a pedantically clean house, they met my request with a swift "no," and promptly returned to their mashed potatoes.

I slunk back to my room to strategize. Never one to take no for an answer, I set about figuring out how I could keep a secret pet all on my own. Could I domesticate a squirrel from the front yard? Too rabies-y. Perhaps a small ant colony in a glass jar? Not cuddly enough.

After writing down a few possibilities on a pad of paper in my room, I went to the kitchen for a snack. I opened up the refrigerator door, scanning for something delectable, when it hit me. I saw a carton of eggs and thought, what about a chicken?!

I asked myself how I could get one of the eggs from the refrigerator to hatch into a fuzzy, yellow, fully fledged petling. Not understanding how fertilization worked, I figured that the only thing keeping a refrigerator egg from turning into a chicken was the fact that it was not being warmed in the nest by its mother. Instead of slowly warming into a baby chick, the eggs in the refrigerator had been cruelly snatched from their mothers, and placed in arrested development in the icy gulag of the refrigerator. Not only would I be owning a pet, I would be saving a life!

I ran back to my closet as quickly as my spindly legs could carry me, and cleared my shoes out of the corner to create a space for the nest. I amassed blankets and towels from various locations around the house, and arranged them delicately in the corner. I snuck back into the kitchen, and furtively plucked the smoothest white egg from the container. I cupped it lovingly in my sweaty palms to begin the warming process that would surely spring my little chick to life within a matter of days. I sat in my closet under the single lightbulb that hung from the ceiling and waited until the egg had reached my body temperature. I then wrapped it up in blanket after blanket, until it resembled an unwieldy cocoon next to my Reebok Pumps. Then I waited. And waited. And waited.

Every day I would unwrap the bundle of blankets to check on my baby chick. "How are you, baby chicken?" I would coo at the lukewarm egg in my palm. Each day, I noticed no discernible change, but figured that all the hard work was happening on the inside. With enough literal and figurative warmth, my baby chick was undoubtedly growing in there and would spring out of their shell any day now.

After about two weeks of watching, waiting, and warming my little egg, I began to worry. What was happening in there? Why was this taking so long? This was a pre-internet era, so I couldn't just ask Google how to raise a refrigerator egg into a chicken, and this was a secret from my parents so I could hardly ask them. My brother was four, and my sister two, so they were useless in terms of chicken raising knowledge. I would just have to wait.

Another few weeks passed, and I diligently held and rewrapped my little egg every night before bed. Then one night I opened up the blanket and I noticed that a funny smell was emanating from my little nest. I clutched my egg with care, and lifted it closer to my nose. It smelled. . .putrid.

I sat woefully in the closet, wondering what had gone wrong. The closet had begun to reek, and I had to know if my little chick was okay in there. I left the egg in the closet and scampered into the kitchen to see if anyone was around. It was dark, and everyone in the house had headed to bed. The coast was clear. I brought my flashlight with me and carried my egg into the kitchen, praying that no one would hear me or smell the odor as I passed their bedrooms. I pulled a bowl out of the cabinet, and decided that this was my moment of truth. I would have to break open the egg and see if the chick was growing in there.

My eyes narrowed as I focused in on the bowl under the dim light of the flashlight. I cracked the side of the egg as gently as I could, but the insides came pouring out in a warm, liquid heap of rancid goo. I gagged. There was no sign of a chicken—just putrid sludge from the world's smelliest rotten egg.

The next day, I licked my wounds and recalibrated. I decided that in order to grow, refrigerator eggs must need not just warmth, but a live body actually sitting on them, and that I was both too heavy and had too busy a school schedule to provide this kind of environment. I needed something simpler.

On a family trip to the beach a few weeks later, I scanned the tidepool at a small outcropping of rocks for anything that looked pet-like. I dragged my red plastic bucket over to a rock covered in barnacle-crusted mussels.

Surely these clam-like creatures would make a suitable pet! With all my might, I wrestled two large mussels from off the rocks and placed them in my bucket. I had filled it with a light layer of sand, a few small rocks, and a few inches of seawater, to mimic its oceanic home. I smuggled the bucket into my parents' car, and hurtled down the freeway toward home.

I settled the mussels in (where else?) my closet, in the corner previously home to my rotten egg. I figured they must be getting hungry by now, but what do mussels eat? Since they are stuck on rocks and ocean water crashes over them all day, I figured they had to eat something in the water—but what could that be? I sat on the pink carpet in my closet, thinking—what could possibly be in ocean water for mussels to eat? I thought and I thought, when it hit me—it had to be salt. So I ran to the kitchen.

I grabbed a small cylinder of iodized salt from the cabinet, hid it under my shirt, and scurried back to my bedroom. I opened the metallic spout, and poured salt into the bucket. "Eat up, little mussels. Grow strong!" I urged. I watched the water grow cloudy with salt, and then suddenly, I noticed, the mussels shells were opening. Slowly, the shells opened, as though their mouths were agape, allowing the salt to pour in.

I jumped up and down in the closet, elated. I had done it! I had figured it out, and fed my pet mussels. They would surely grow large and strong in my closet—my secret pets. I reached in to stroke one of their shells, and went outside to play.

The next morning, I noticed that the mussels shells remained opened. Could they still be eating the salt I had put in there? That seemed like a very long feeding. As the days wore on, their shells never closed again, and soon my closet started to reek once more—this time, of rotting seafood. I would later learn that mussels open when they die (that's why they open when you cook them), and instead of feeding them with salt, I had rendered their environment completely uninhabitable by pouring in their "food."

I never did get a pet, though on my journey I managed to accidentally kill a jar of sea monkeys (brine shrimp, for the uninitiated), overfeed a neighborhood cat that I later learned belonged to a woman down the street, and briefly keep a baby bird that had fallen from its nest on life support before it succumbed to its injuries.

I wish that the moral of that story was that anything is possible if you work hard enough (it's not). Or that if you keep trying, eventually you will succeed (another cruel lie from childhood inspirational posters). What I can tell you is that this absurdly high level of unassailable hope, coupled with the stubbornness to keep trying in the face of abject failure, is absolutely what it takes to start a business in America.

Every year, we have holidays that celebrate dead presidents, war veterans, and a potpourri of American icons. Given that American small businesses create most of the jobs in our economy, I want to know why there isn't a holiday for the everyday people who keep the lights on in this place—especially because, in my estimation, you have to be a goddamn genius to navigate getting your doors open.

I have done some challenging things widely acknowledged as requiring a big-ass brain, and none of them were as mentally taxing as figuring out how to open a postage-stamp-sized restaurant. I was an attorney, for God's sake, and I damn near gave up trying to figure out how to navigate the minefield of laws and government approvals required to open a macaroni and cheese restaurant in Oakland.

> *This absurdly high level of unassailable hope, coupled with the stubbornness to keep trying in the face of abject failure, is absolutely what it takes to start a business in America.*

First up, there is a maze of corporate paperwork with the secretary of state, the IRS, the US Patent and Trademark Office, and a host of other obscurely acronymed entities to do things like name your company or scratch your elbow. Figuring out their forms was so complicated that I, a lawyer, had to hire another lawyer who specialized in this area, to help.

Then I had to get approval from the health department, which made such health-saving additions to my plans as requiring a $20,000 fully plumbed closet with specially cleanable walls so that we could temporarily store garbage if we were too lazy to take it to the dumpster. I was not sure why we would put garbage in a closet for any period of time instead of just taking it directly outside, but they insisted. After opening, we installed coat hooks in the $20,000 closet and turned it into, well, a closet.

Then I had to register with the California State Board of Equalization, on whose behalf we would collect nearly 10 percent in sales tax on every purchase. The problem is that not all items are taxable, and it was nearly impossible to figure out which ones were and which ones weren't. For instance, a drink with ice in it is taxable, but a cold drink with no ice is not. In an abundance of caution, I added tax to every item we sold out of abject fear that we would get it wrong, because in an audit we would be held accountable for messing up. Years later, we were still fined $10,000 in an audit because we gave staff free beers at the end of their shift, and apparently we should have been collecting sales tax on the free beer we were giving away. Silly me.

And don't even get me started on what it takes to sell a beer. An incomplete list of things that are easier to do in America than get a permit to sell a beer: buy a semi-automatic gun, get a driver's license, start your own tax-free religion, foster a child, import an exotic animal. First, I was fingerprinted and subjected to a background check more rigorous than the one required when I worked at the US Attorney's Office. Then I had to notify my neighbors and attend a hearing because one of them complained that if my restaurant served alcohol, it would contribute to an increase in the local rodent population.

I had to pore through hundreds of numbered designations and figure out which of all the freakishly similar permits I needed to apply for that applied to a restaurant that has beer on the menu. Is it Type 41, "On Sale Beer and Wine Eating Place," or Type 42, "On Sale Beer and Wine Public Premises"? Or perhaps Type 47, "On Sale General Eating Place"? The list is so specific and varied that it includes such gems as Type 62, "On Sale General Bona Fide Public Eating Place Intermittent Dockside Vessel," and Type 88, "Special On Sale General License for a For-Profit Cemetery with Specified Characteristics." I could not figure out what half of these words even meant (what is "on sale"?), let alone whether they applied to me. I ultimately threw a dart at the word salad of all the licenses that didn't involve cemeteries and dockside vessels, and crossed my fingers I had landed on the right one

Experienced restaurateurs generally hire someone to wade through the administrative thicket of beer and wine licenses, and the going rates begin at $10,000. This is after spending anywhere from $4,000 to $150,000 on the license itself, and the process can take anywhere from a bare minimum of six months to countless years if multiple neighbors complain. This is what it took to sell one kind of drink on my menu.

I had begun my quest to open a mac and cheese restaurant with what seemed like an ungodly sum of money to me at the time—all the savings I had in the world—but amid all the costly bureaucracy, the expenses just kept ballooning. I didn't have the kind of budget that could support even one $20,000 closet, but at that point I was so deep into the project I couldn't turn back. So I did what generations of reckless Americans have done when they can't afford shit—I racked up wild amounts of credit card debt.

I applied for every credit card I could get my hands on to pay for things I could never have imagined in my wildest entrepreneurial nightmares. Continuing conversations with the health department led to $5,000 of specially coated shelving for boxes to sit on, a $10,000 oven that could ingest its own steam (not sure how steam afflicts public health, but this was the only way around a $100,000 ventilation system required to do the same thing, which I was later required to install anyway), sinks for every occasion (because God forbid someone washes a dish under a faucet later used to rinse a carrot). Is this what all people who own restaurants had to go through to open them? How was there even one single functioning restaurant in all of California?

As I watched my bank account dive down faster than a seagull who has spotted a discarded French fry, I realized that I would need to find a partner who could infuse additional cash to get Homeroom open. I didn't know anyone crazy enough to join me on this endeavor, so I asked literally the only other person I knew who wanted to open a restaurant—a woman named Allison—if she wanted to join me. We had met at a cafe a few months earlier and had since bonded over our mutual love of restaurants. Much to my surprise, she said yes.

While we would later part ways and she would go on to open an Italian restaurant in New York, Allison's willingness to put her time and money into an idea even my own family was unwilling to fund gave my spirits a massive boost. Homeroom would not have gotten its doors open without her—not just her cash, but her belief in me and my bizarre dream of creating a dairy-filled mecca, not to mention her husband's carpentry skills when we ran out of money yet again.

Since there was no money left to pay the contractor to seal the floors, I watched YouTube tutorials to figure out how to do it myself. This involved renting a power washer to clean the concrete, with a spray hose so powerful it catapulted my bodyweight backwards when I turned it on. After waiting a few days for it to dry, I spread the floor with a potent polyurethane sealant that had to be rolled on with a giant paint roller, coating the floor with a clear sheen as it sprayed noxious fumes into the air. I didn't want to invest in specialty shoes so instead did the job in my fuzzy pink bedtime socks. Then, unable to locate an industrial air blower to dry the floor, I attempted to dry it inch by inch with a handheld blow-dryer in my fuzzy socks.

Because I had no money to hire professionals or buy things like furniture, much of the work of building Homeroom looked exactly like this. Instead of ordering chairs like a normal person, I had to Craigslist dozens of chairs being given away for free, then rent a U-Haul to go pick them up from an obscure location 50 miles away. I wandered into a low-slung warehouse in a suburban strip mall, and for a moment feared that this is where I had come to die. It was filled with decrepit junk, and the barren building was barely lit by a few dangling fluorescent lights. A heavyset man in a stained T-shirt came to greet me, and I began to panic that I had just wandered into an empty building with a lone man who had lured me there with the offer of free things. What had I done? Thankfully, he barely acknowledged my existence and brought me over to the stash of free chairs. They were hideous.

Since I was now the empress of the home renovation online tutorial, I researched how to de-uglify these chairs. I figured out that they just needed to be stained and resealed, but my first chair took me the better part of a day to complete. I needed to do this to 75 chairs. At my current rate, this would take me four months to complete—and this was just the chairs. We still needed tables, a bar, shelving, painted walls. I had reached the absolute limit of my credit and was denied any additional cards or increase in credit. I went to a dozen banks to see if I could apply for a loan, but most would not provide loans to restaurants given the risk profile of the industry, and those that would require collateral like a house, which I didn't have.

I was complaining to my brother Stephen about my predicament, when he told me about a new website called Kickstarter. It was for raising money for various projects, and had just recently been launched. I began poring through the website, and was inspired by all the quirky projects people were launching around the world. With calls to action like "Help build the world's best psychedelic beer cozy!" the site was filled with earnest eccentrics trying to bring their ideas to life. It's hard to imagine now when Kickstarter projects regularly raise over a million dollars, but those early projects were much more modest. The idea of asking strangers for money was so new that the thought of raising a million dollars was downright laughable—most projects were for a few thousand. I set my sights on raising $5,000.

I put together an amateur video on my laptop, offered outlandishly generous prizes like gift boxes in exchange for relatively paltry donations, and crossed my fingers. Homeroom ended up being the first restaurant to successfully raise money on Kickstarter, and we raised nearly $9,000. More importantly, there were now hundreds of followers from around the world that seemed to genuinely care whether or not we opened this thing. Using the funds to purchase things like used bleacher wood as lumber for the furniture, I sent out a call for help getting things rolling. Complete strangers materialized like angels from up above to help paint walls and sand those ugly-ass chairs. Friends and family also showed up in droves, and all the tables, shelves, and bar were made by hand with love.

After months of these DIY project-filled workdays on everything from creating light fixtures to carving a wood sign, the final touches were being put on the space. I was so broke that after a friend drove 350 miles from LA for the opening party and asked for a T-shirt, I had to charge him for it. That shirt represented an hour's worth of labor that I couldn't afford to give away. Homeroom had a mere two weeks of operating expenses in its account. Two weeks! So even after all of the community support, a year of my life, the permits, the inspections, the equipment, and all my life savings and credit on the line—if Homeroom wasn't an immediate success, it would be an immediate failure.

It was like walking into my childhood closet after weeks with my egg—tending to it, loving it, keeping it warm. Wanting so desperately for this thing to come alive. I could only hope that my skills in birthing a business were better than my knack for nurturing pets. It was time to crack the egg open and see what was inside.

11 | Hiring

The Eerie Resemblance Between Hiring and Dating

"True leadership isn't about having an idea. It's about having an idea and recruiting other people to execute on this vision."

—*Leila Janah*

My first kiss was during a game of seventh-grade spin the bottle. As I watched the bottle twirl round and round, I prayed for it to land on one of my crushes as my heart pounded so hard in my chest I worried others could hear it. My energy deflated when the bottle landed on a bespectacled boy with a bowl cut from my biology class, whose favorite pastime was making raptor noises behind me on the bus. The kiss was brief yet somehow damp, a cumbersome entry into adolescence.

The awkwardness of this first encounter, my blind hope for something magical, and the randomness of the outcome set the appropriate stage for years of dating to come. Growing up watching a steady stream of 1980s rom-coms had prepared me for this. What they had not prepared me for was the fact that romantic dating is not the only kind of dating that those in search of a happy ending must endure. The other kind—the kind none of us can choose to avoid—is the job interview.

The premise of romantic dating and job dating (aka interviews) is almost identical: two strangers sit in a room and have a conversation to decide if they can see a future together. They are stuck relying on conversation and affect as shitty stand-ins for the truth about what it will be like to collaborate in a meaningful way. Each party looks for cues in the other, searching for meaning behind each detail. If someone is late, red flags are raised about reliability. If someone starts talking shit about a former employer or partner, alarm bells go off around trustworthiness. We try to guess based on outfit and appearance whether someone is organized or messy and search their past experiences for signs of competence, intelligence, and drive.

I've always thought that both job interviews and dates are not good for sussing out who will be a good match but can be helpful in figuring out who is not. Like, you don't know if the person who is perfectly normal in conversation will be a good partner, but you do know that the person who yells obscenities at the barista before insulting your outfit choice will probably not be.

My interview at the law firm back when I was a fresh-faced attorney was just such a red-flag date. Like, I should have known better, but they were totally loaded and looked good to my parents, so I pressed forward anyway. The firm was the legal equivalent of dating a millionaire (billionaire?)—the lobby was filled with overstuffed leather chairs overlooking the glistening ocean and the Golden Gate Bridge. They paid their summer associates much more for a ten-week stint than I made all year as a chef.

Mike, the guy who interviewed me, was a partner at the firm. He had married his former summer associate, which was the first red flag at a firm that represented employers being sued for things like sleeping with subordinates at work.

I walked awkwardly into Mike's office, my footfall unsteady in the high heels I dusted off solely for job interviews and weddings. Red flag number two: if you need to wear an outfit that makes you want to die in order be accepted, maybe this is not an ideal working relationship.

"Welcome, Erin," Mike pronounced loudly, from behind his oversized desk, and gestured at a chair opposite him. "Take a seat." His neatly cropped blond hair was slicked back, his eyes fixed on paperwork.

The premise of romantic dating and job dating (aka interviews) is almost identical: two strangers sit in a room and have a conversation to decide if they can see a future together. They are stuck relying on conversation and affect as shitty stand-ins for the truth about what it will be like to collaborate in a meaningful way.

I sat down gingerly, eyeing the collection of thick legal books and awards on the shelf behind him, alongside trophies featuring large gavels and open books, which reminded me of being in a nerdy fourth grader's bedroom.

"First things first," he said, cracking open my file, which sat in front of him. "Why the mediocre LSAT score?"

"Excuse me?" I asked. I had never been in an interview with such an aggressive opening question. I was used to softballs, like "Tell me about yourself," or "Why do you picture yourself here?"

"You heard me," he countered. "Your LSAT score—it sucks. Why?"

"Um . . ." I stammered. I couldn't believe he was asking me about my law school admissions test. What did that have to do with anything? Plus, I was attending one of the best law schools in the country, so obviously someone thought my score was okay. "I don't know if you noticed, but I took it twice. I flubbed it the first time, but then did considerably better the second."

"Why did you flub it?" he pressed.

"I'm not the best with standardized tests. I studied like crazy and brought it up to be in the top 5 percent of scores."

"But Erin," he looked me straight in the eye, "this is a top 1 percent law firm. We only want the best. Was this your best?"

Mike's tone was accusatory—angry, even. If my LSAT score had put me out of the running for this job, I could not figure out why I had even been invited to this interview.

"Well, yes—that was my best." I answered, suppressing my rage. He didn't know it, but standardized tests were something I had struggled with my entire short life. They were the gatekeepers to a lot of places I wanted to go, but no matter how hard I tried, my scores never reflected what I thought were my capabilities. I bought every possible study guide, took every practice test that existed, only to either bomb or score in the lowest possible range that schools I was looking at would consider. The first year I applied to law school, I didn't get into a single school, despite having graduated at the top of my class from one of the fanciest colleges in the country. I had to study at nights after work for a second year in a row, retake the LSAT, and reapply to all the same schools again a year later with my higher score—a score that I had worked my ass off for and was now being mocked in this interview.

"If this is your best, what makes you think you belong here?" Mike asked.

I thought long and hard. Fuck this guy.

"Because I'm doing well now in one of the best law schools. That seems more relevant than the test I took to get in there."

"Okay," Mike replied, "but doesn't this test demonstrate how you perform under pressure? I'm not sure you could handle it here."

What the fuck was his problem? And were we ever going to move off this stupid topic?

"I can handle pressure just fine," I replied, clenching my hands. My mind frame shifted from trying to get the job to just getting the hell out of Mike's office.

"I see from your résumé that you've done a lot of courtroom work, so perhaps that's true. Court is an intense environment," Mike said.

Thank God, I thought. I was ready to move on into the part of the interview where we discussed the possibility that I might actually be good at this job. Instead, Mike grilled me with every possible inadequacy he could find in my résumé, my writing sample, my life. By the end, my mood flipped between feeling despondent and punchy. Part of me wanted to vindicate myself and get this guy's approval—the other part of me just wanted to punch him in the face. Finally, he signaled it was almost over.

"Last question—you've done all public interest and government work. Do-gooder stuff. Why should I believe that you'd be in it for the long haul here? That you're not just in it to make a quick buck and go on to do other things? What guarantee do I have that if we invest in you, you'll stick around?"

The quick buck he mentioned was exactly why I was in his office. In most interviews I would have come up with some flowery reason why the job I was interviewing for represented my deepest passion, but I had run out of fucks to give.

"Well, sir," I said, leaning in closer to his desk, "I guess you don't have any guarantee."

And that was it.

Two days later, I was stunned to discover that I had gotten the job. Mike called me personally to congratulate me and mentioned that he had been impressed by my no-bullshit attitude. Apparently, I was the first person to have answered that last question honestly, which he admired. I didn't understand it at the time, but his dickwad approach was a common interview style at law firms, intended to rattle the candidate and see how they perform under pressure. Apparently I kept my cool despite the rage that was boiling under my surface.

First dates—I mean, job interviews—do tell you a lot about who you are getting involved with. At the law firm, the interview was designed to test how much abuse I could withstand and how well I could keep my cool. That would prove a vital skill for survival there, and one that defined my time with that employer. Similarly, my daylong, unpaid interviews for kitchen jobs tested how hard I was willing to work for little to no pay— which was an honest foreshadowing of the work that lay ahead in that realm.

I hated these jobs, along with the interviews that led to them. So when it came time to hire at Homeroom, I obsessed over how to do better. If I was creating my own dream job but everyone who came to work with me dreaded being there, the endeavor would feel like a failure. I wanted to create a place that felt good not just for me, but for everyone who worked there. The only problem was, I had no idea how to do it.

I have scoured the internet to find the text of Homeroom's first job post, to no avail. But its utopian promise went a little something like this:

> Do you crave work that you actually want to wake up and do each day? So do we. Please join us in building a legitimately fun, connecting, and delicious restaurant together. You don't need to have restaurant experience, just a love of great food and working with people. We are building a restaurant dedicated to the world's best food—macaroni and cheese—and are looking to build a family of food lovers to make it the best possible place to work and eat. Please join us at our open interviews to introduce yourself and find out more—this Saturday from eight to ten.

My idea was to hold open interviews in the restaurant space, which was still under construction. I thought that an open-house format would set a casual and friendly tone, where candidates could come by, see the space, and sit down with me over coffee. On the morning of the open house, a line began forming early outside the front door. It was a chilly winter morning in the Bay Area, and folks were warming their hands with their breath, and bopping up and down to stay warm. I wanted to invite them inside, except that the line kept growing with each passing minute. I had anticipated a few dozen people showing up in the two-hour time window, but there were already a few dozen waiting, with dozens more streaming down the sidewalk toward the line. I counted 30, then 50, then 70, and then over 150 by the time the interviews were about to begin.

Panic began to set in around the 60-person mark, when I realized that my approach of having a chill coffee with candidates would not work. Sixty candidates in two hours meant that I would have two minutes per person, and the line had since ballooned to almost three times that number of people—so approximately one minute per person. Fuck. This was not the beautiful beginning of the utopian ideal I had imagined. I was about to be a really, really bad date. I stared at the laughably small tray of cookies I had waiting for everyone (at current count, each person could have .18 of a cookie) and wanted to throw up.

After doing some raw math on the back of an invoice, I started furiously scribbling numbers on a pile of notecards I had brought with me. I walked out to address the line.

"Hi everyone!" I screamed, trying to reach those in line way down the block, "I'm Erin! The owner. I can't tell you how grateful I am to you for showing up. This turnout far, far exceeds what I had imagined in my wildest dreams. I had planned on doing casual interviews over the course of a few hours, but obviously that won't work for this number of people. We can't even all fit into the restaurant, and I know it's a really cold day. I'm going to hand out numbers to everyone in line, and interview everyone in order for five minutes. You all deserve much more time than that, but with this number of people even just five minutes per person will take ten hours to get through. I understand if you can't wait or come back, and if so, you're welcome to drop your résumé off with me. If not, you can use your number to figure out a rough time to return. If I have missed your number, I'm happy to take you later whenever you make it back. I will stay here as long as it takes to interview everyone. I am so sorry for how inconvenient this is, and am so very appreciative of you coming here today."

About 30 people pulled out of line immediately and handed me their résumé, and of the 120 people who remained, about half remained lined up down the block, with the other half leaving to return later in the day.

The five-minute interview was like speed-dating—before I could get any real information about anyone I was on to the next. Some people made it easy—one candidate named Ryan began the interview by handing me a coffee he had purchased for me. "This is a long day for you," he said. "I thought you could use a little pick-me-up," he said, placing the warm cup in my hand. While most candidates were concerned with how they appeared in the interview, Ryan was showing me how he would do the job, by providing kind and thoughtful service.

Other candidates were harder to judge, and the five-minute interview did no one any favors. One woman teared up about being unemployed, another man spoke in halting and broken English about washing dishes. I never got to learn anything further about either one. A bubbly server promoted her ability to sell onion rings, while a local homeless man wandered in for the free snacks. Hours passed in five-minute increments, with waves of nervous people moving in and out of the seat in front of me. I must have passed over countless introverts, and great candidates who needed more of a warmup than the single question we had time for. I overhired for charisma, one of the few things that you can assess in a short period of time but that, I would later learn, is also the most common foil for incompetence.

By the end of the day, my brain was overloaded with tiny details about dozens of brief and unsatisfying encounters. I felt lost as to what factors to give weight to, so relied heavily on my instinct, which is probably the only method less accurate at predicting successful outcomes than standardized testing. I slunk into my chair, reviewing note cards with candidates' names and scant details about their job experience scrawled beneath them. I agonized over them, anguishing over what would happen to those I didn't have space for in the midst of such a dismal job market. I finally selected the top fourteen, an eclectic mix of people from all walks of life in the city.

I picked up my phone to call Ryan first. He picked up on the first ring.

"Hello?" he said.

"Hi, Ryan. It's Erin, from the interview today."

"Oh yeah!" he said, "I'm so glad you called."

"Me too," I said, eager to relate the good news. "I would love to work with you."

If you're going on a first date and want to show you're romantic or generous, bring a small gift. If you're interviewing for a job in hospitality—show hospitality.

"Yeah?" he said. After such a long day sitting with anxious people, it was a relief to hear palpable joy.

"Yeah!" I called back. "I was so moved that you brought me coffee—thank you for that."

"Well, I just figured that food makes everything better," he said.

"It sure does."

I made a lot of stupid decisions that day, but Ryan was one of the best hires I ever made. Ryan worked at Homeroom for many years before departing to open a restaurant with his wife, who fell for him during her days as a Homeroom regular. No one has since brought me a coffee to a job interview, but if I can offer a word of wisdom—they should. If you're going on a first date and want to show you're romantic or generous, bring a small gift. If you're interviewing for a job in hospitality—show hospitality. I'll take a good coffee over a conversation about how skilled you are at serving coffee every time.

12 | Rulemaking

On Trying Not to Become Your Parents

"I love rules and I love following them, unless that rule is stupid."
—*Anna Kendrick*

When I was in high school, I had an imaginary best friend named Danielle Darling. There was a real Danielle Darling at my school—a cheerleader with meticulous blond highlights and a boyfriend who resembled a Latino Ken doll. The real Danielle had no idea that I existed, yet she unwittingly played a critical role in my high school social life.

Every Saturday of senior year, I would tell my parents I was at a sleepover at Danielle's house. I posted her parents' phone number up on my parents' fridge, and shuffled awkwardly out the door into the dry LA evening, an electric tingle under my skin.

I would head straight to my boyfriend Ben's house—he occupied the entire basement of his dad's house following his parents' bitter divorce. His father, a schleppy Jewish man with a slow gait, was delighted that his son had a Jewish girlfriend and turned a blind eye to our Saturday night sleepovers. Ben and I would stay up late listening to the Dave Matthews Band on repeat, staring at the fake stars on his ceiling, and exchanging deep thoughts about the upcoming X-Men movie.

The phone number I had left on my parents' fridge was actually my friend Nina's father's fax number. This was an era of digital dinosaurs, where fax lines and phone lines did double duty, so it wasn't unusual to call a phone number and get a busy signal that a fax was being sent.

My parents tried to call Danielle a few times to check up on me, but every time they got a fax signal. I told them that her dad worked from home, and he must just be really busy—because, you know, Saturday nights are when most people are up late doing their best work. Since I came home promptly on Sunday mornings, my parents didn't seem overly invested in the late night work habits of Danielle's father.

At the time, I was not allowed to have boys in my room with the door closed. (Too bad I later discovered I was gay and those closed-door girl sessions could have really been a boon to my teenage love life.) My parents would have grounded me for an eternity if they had found out I was sleeping over with a boy, so I invented Danielle to escape certain punishment.

Conjuring an imaginary best friend to escape punishment for a rule I didn't understand or respect had left a mark. I wanted my parents to respect my judgment and autonomy, and I was jealous of my friends' parents with more lax rules about sleepovers. I told myself that when I was in a position

91

of authority one day, I would do it differently. I wouldn't adhere to social convention just because that is the way most people do it. I would include other people in decision-making, respect what they had to say, and find ways to honor both of our needs.

Our first staff meeting at Homeroom had 14 people, all sitting on barstools around a 16-foot-long communal table built from old bleacher wood. The surface of the wood was littered with seat numbers, which reminded me of sitting on crisp evenings at high school football games where the real Danielle Darling would be cheering on the sidelines.

"Welcome, everyone," I said, as the nervous chatter died down. "I am so excited you're here. Let's go around the table and introduce ourselves— maybe we can start with your name, the job you were hired to do, and one thing about yourself you find interesting."

"Hi, I'm Ryan," said my soft-spoken coffee mate, looking crisp in fitted suspenders and a blue beanie. "I was hired as a server, and something inter-esting about me is that I just moved here from San Diego. Homeroom is the first business I passed on my way into town. When I saw the posters in the window, somehow I knew I was supposed to work here." Ryan looked nervously down at the table, shifting the group's focus to the woman next to him.

"I'm Desiree, but you can call me Dre," a smiling young woman said, tucking a strand of stray hair behind a bright pink bandanna. "I'll be work-ing in the kitchen, and a fun fact about me is that the secret to my mama's mac and cheese recipe is a healthy dose of Velveeta. I'll bring y'all some one day."

Folks were sweet, earnest, and nervous going around the table. There was Omar, who was recently out of prison for a crime I never asked about, but he still wore an ankle bracelet tracking his movements. Tiffany, a bubbly server who resembled Pippi Longstocking in both her dress and demeanor. Martin, a middle-aged father of two who had always dreamed of being a chef but had never worked in a kitchen before. Diego, whose baby face looked 13 but who had just turned 18, and Homeroom was his first job. Darius, a consummate charmer with swagger so big it filled a room. Mick, the lead in a local punk band.

After going through the logistics of our first event—a Valentine's Day mac and cheese tasting dinner two days away—I opened the floor for questions.

"What are we supposed to wear? Is there a uniform?" Dre asked.

"Nope, no uniform. I want you to be yourself—just wear whatever feels comfortable," I said.

Diego's hand shot up, "Boss, I have a question."

Boss, I thought. *Who is that?*

"Yes, Diego," I replied, trying to suppress my surprise at my new title.

"But what about shoes—like shouldn't we not wear things like flip-flops?"

"Yeah," Tiffany said. "That would be dangerous."

"Okay," I said, "No flip-flops, I guess. I mean, use your best judgment. I trust you."

"But what about shirts with inappropriate words on them?" Martin asked. "Wouldn't that offend customers? Or other staff?"

"Well," I said, my confidence diminishing by the second, "I guess that's part of using your judgment. Don't wear something you think might offend people."

"But what happens if we do?" Mick asked, suppressing a grin, "Will we get in trouble?"

"No," I replied, though I was unsure what I would actually do in such a situation. "We would probably just have a conversation about it. I mean, it seems like you all have really good ideas about safety and appropriate clothing for work. We're all grownups here—I trust you."

"But what about people who show up for work looking messy?" asked Darius, "I worked at a place where this one server always had dirty hair and smelled. It was disgusting, and makes us all look bad."

"I trust you all to shower, and show up for work clean," I said.

"But what happens if someone doesn't?" asked Mick.

Things did not improve as we moved onto the Homeroom vacation policy.

"So our vacation policy is that there is no vacation policy. You are all adults who know when you need a break, so take one when you need one." I announced.

Crickets.

After an awkward pause, Diego's hand shot up, "But Boss, what if everyone wants to take vacation at the same time?"

Boss again—this is gonna take me a while to get used to, I thought.

"I don't think that's going to happen," I said.

"Well, it could," inserted Martin, "What if it's a holiday we all want off?"

"I guess we'll have to decide what holidays we close for," I said, my head spinning with all of the potential closures I had failed to account for in my already tenuous financial models.

"But, like, won't everyone just want to take Saturdays off?" asked Dre.

"Well, I guess that's possible," I considered. "Although tips are higher on weekends, right? So won't some people still want to work?"

"What if it's not enough people?" inquired Tiffany, "Then it will just be overwhelming for everyone who's still working."

We went on like this for about 30 minutes, at which point I beleaguredly repeated my mantra that was intended to be empowering but in reality proved anxiety-provoking, "Don't worry—I trust you."

What the fuck was going on? Why weren't people stoked for this? In all the jobs I had ever had, I was dying for my bosses to give me the kind of autonomy and trust I was lavishing on my new staff, and all they wanted was. . .rules.

The tenor of the first staff meeting left my nerves frayed, but our opening event for Valentine's Day was a smashing success. Our dinner was a welcome counterpoint to the stuffy, overpriced, and formulaic disasters that Valentine's Day dinners normally look like. Groups of friends and couples on dates filled the booths and gobbled up course after course of smothered cheesy noodles paired with local beer and wine. There was a dim glow from candles on the tables, a local band playing softly in the background, and the hum of great conversation filling the room. The event felt special, yet approachable— exactly what I wanted every night at Homeroom to feel like. Unfortunately, we were destined not to have another one like it for quite some time.

We had presold tickets to the Valentine's event, which limited the number of people we were serving. When we arrived the next morning to prepare for opening, a line of customers had already formed down the entire length of the block and opening was still hours away. There were more people waiting in that line already than we had served the entire night before.

"That's a lot of people, Boss," said Diego, staring out the window while tying his apron around his waist.

"I know," I replied.

"We went through a lot of food last night," said Omar, checking the fridges. "I think we'll need more prep for the morning."

"On it!" called Dre, pouring bags of elbow pasta into a vat of boiling water.

The staff was buzzing, the kitchen a swirl of boiling pasta and shredded cheese, while the servers cleaned the remains of the night's party.

Since I had never hired anyone before, hiring an initial staff of 14 had felt like a huge and intimidating number to me. Unfortunately, in the weeks and months to come, I would learn that that number bordered on negligence—Homeroom required a staff of 50, not 14, to run properly. So even being fully staffed that first day, we were a football team short of players and the air was thick with panic.

When our doors finally opened, the line was three blocks long, and I could not even see the end of it. I hastily took our first dollar from our first customer—a proud father with a gleaming smile and his six-year old daughter, who handed me the bill with a wide grin. I gave her a homemade Oreo cookie to thank her for her patience, tacked the bill up on the wall, then sprinted back to the kitchen to help stir pots of mac and cheese for the hungry hordes.

If you have ever been at a short-staffed restaurant, it feels like being Moses crossing the desert, trying to figure out how to reach the promised land of lunch. Filthy tables sat abandoned as hangry customers lingered near the doorway trying to make eye contact with harried staff. The servers and bussers were barely containing a sprint as they moved through the restaurant, juggling dishes, orders, and the dashed hopes and dreams of customers seeking their favorite dish we just ran out of. The cluttered entryway became littered with an increasingly desperate, eye-contact-seeking mob, trying to figure out how to score a table in this godforsaken place. Simple things like paying the bill became an exercise in stalking.

Some choice thoughts from our Yelp reviewers at the time:

"All the staff was banging into each other—it was almost entertaining to watch. Like a Greek tragedy."

—*Joel B.*

"The current system is controlled chaos; a long line of camera-strapped foodies snaking through the crowded restaurant."

—*Kris G.*

"Trying to pick up our take-out order was a complete clusterfuck."

—*Eileen R.*

My utopian work rules merely added to the madness. Since no one had a uniform, guests would flag down random customers returning from the bathroom to get them water, because they couldn't tell who was an employee and who was just a hip-looking passerby. Our kitchen crew resembled a motley band of misfits from a weird mash-up of punk, hip-hop, and Banda music videos. They would alternate blasting their favorite music and I would overhear customers gawking disapprovingly into our open kitchen from the sidewalk. It turns out that when it comes to food preparation, this is not a place where guests want to see personality—they want things to look uniform, clean, and really, really boring.

That first day, we ran out of food after serving about 300 people, and sent the remaining ones home with free cookies to soften the blow. The team and I had labored for nearly 15 hours, and resembled the walking dead. After all the money was counted, the floors swept, and the staff briefed on suggestions for the next day, I slouched in a seat nursing a beer. Dre, Ryan, and Mick joined me, pouring their favorite drinks from the tap.

"Boss," said Diego, tapping me on the shoulder on his way out, "I think that Tiffany is in the bathroom crying."

"Crying?" I asked.

"Crying," he said. "She says the way we take orders is not emotionally fulfilling."

Fabulous, I thought, wondering what the hell that even meant and trying to summon the energy to stand up and check on her.

"Before you get up," Dre said, "I think we're not going to have enough cheese prepped for tomorrow. What should we do?"

"Get everyone here earlier?" I replied, unsure of my own suggestion.

"We're already getting here at 6:00. We need more people—I think we need to ask the servers to help." replied Dre.

"I don't know how thrilled the servers will be to do kitchen prep at 6:00 in the morning after such a brutal day." I added.

"I agree," said Dre, "But I don't see another choice. We'd have to get our kitchen crew here at 4:00 if not. I think we need to hire more people."

"Okay then," I said, beginning to gnaw on one of my fingernails. "I will call the servers and ask them to come in early to help out in the kitchen."

I could not imagine what kind of masochist would be willing to say yes. The delta between the glorious workplace I had promised in my job posting and the reality on the ground was stark.

"Sure thing," Dre said, managing somehow to squeeze out a smile.

My legs throbbed from standing all day, and all I wanted was to go home and sleep, but my mind was racing. We had killed ourselves today, and would have to somehow manage to pull off this crazy stunt again tomorrow, and then the day after that. It felt like deciding to run back-to-back marathons when injured, knowing that at some point you'll be unable to run, let alone walk. I was so grateful that we had business—that would have been the only true disaster, given the pennies left in my bank account—but if we couldn't figure out how to make Homeroom feel like less of a circus, then I couldn't imagine our lines would persist for long.

13 | Mission

The Only Good Reason to Change out of Soft Pants in the Morning

> "We all have ability. The difference is how we use it."
>
> —*Stevie Wonder*

The power of lard brought my parents together. The day my parents met, my American father was visiting Israel, standing outside a movie theatre, eating an entire box of Oreos by himself. This was back in the day that the Oreo filling was peak delicious owing to the fact that Nabisco used lard to make the sugary white center (it has since been replaced by vegetable shortening to cater to Jews, vegetarians, and all other non-pig-eating people). As such, the cookies were not kosher for Jews to eat, and rarely found on the streets of Jerusalem.

My mother approached my father to ask for a cookie, which he gladly shared, not realizing what precious contraband he was holding. As they struck up a conversation, she learned that not only was he an Oreo-eating goy, but that he had grown up in the ultimate unkosher profession—a pig farmer from America.

They shared the box of cookies throughout the movie, my mom dipping her hands into the box for the forbidden treats. And so began a relationship that would span more than 50 years, and an untold number of pork products.

Being raised in the home of an Israeli Jew and American pig farmer, I experienced a mash-up of both cultures. Specifically, I was raised to deliver Jewish hospitality featuring American food. If you're unfamiliar with Jewish hospitality, the main idea is to ply guests with food immediately upon their arrival, and then consistently until they leave. And by guests, I mean anyone who comes to the door. The visitor could be a neighbor, a parent picking up their child from a playdate, or a pesky Jehovah's Witness; regardless, Jewish hospitality insists that you invite them in and feed them something—preferably lots of things—straight away.

My mom would always offer guests hot tea or coffee and serve it on her best china. There was always a stash of homemade baked goods on the counter that my dad had made—chocolate chip cookies loaded with double the chips, gooey chocolate brownies, walnut-studded fudge. A tray of baked treats would accompany the tea, along with an assortment of cheeses stocked in the fridge for exactly this purpose, along with dried fruit, nuts, and other savory snacks.

I have heard that this way of caring for others is born of being a desert people who relied on hospitality to survive harsh living conditions and perilous travel. Another take is that generations of persecution created a culture of caretaking. I'm not sure where the truth lies, but growing up predominantly around the Jews, Persians, Asians, and Latinos who populated my LA public schools, I have found similar traditions among many cultures.

I didn't realize that such warm, food-rich hospitality was not the norm until I went to college and found myself surrounded by very lovely but very Waspy people. Despite the wild amounts of wealth that your average Princeton student was raised with, it was normal to go to a classmate's home and be offered either nothing upon entering, or maybe a glass of water. In a Jewish home, this would be tantamount to giving a visitor the finger or slamming the door in their face.

In those chaotic early days, the thing that kept the lights on was the way we took care of people. Even though we bungled basic things like getting orders out in a timely fashion, we excelled at making up for it in every way that we could think of. What we lacked in staffing and systems, we made up for with heart and a flotilla of free desserts for customers, and a bar's worth of free drinks for staff. (Remember that $10,000 fine? It was on $30,000 of free beer for staff.)

A lot of people think that Homeroom's meteoric success was based on serving exceptional mac and cheese, but I believe it was largely rooted in our exceptional hospitality. While I had no experience as a server, I did have experience with a Jewish mother. I knew that particularly while we were chronically understaffed and figuring out how to run things, we needed to find ways to feed people early and often.

I always thought that an overlooked part of the dining experience is before you have even been seated. The best service you can hope for at a restaurant if there is a wait for a table is to be directed to a bar, where you can buy a drink. This is bullshit. At Homeroom, we made sure to take care of them right away. We would bring glasses of water to guests who were waiting for a table, or mugs of hot tea in the wintertime. These gestures cost us next to nothing, but made people feel cared for because it was a time that they were used to being overlooked. When customers had to endure long waits, this reminded them that we noticed them, and that we were glad they were there.

We all just want to be seen, to be acknowledged—whether we are doing something big like going on a first date or simply waiting for a table. At most restaurants, people are basically ignored until they have purchased something, which communicates that their money is what makes them worthy of attention. The level of gratitude I experienced from guests offered water while waiting for a table was greater than most other gestures I made, including ones that actually cost me money, like sending out a free dish to a table. The surprise of being cared for in a moment when people least expected it felt special. I had multiple customers hug me, and even a few who teared up when I handed them a cup of ice water when they were sweating in the sunshine or a mug of hot tea on a chilly evening. We would even bring over a dog bowl with water for those dining with their pooches. Those tiny gestures that show that you're paying attention to someone else are often the most profound.

We would also collect items throughout the evening that would have normally been thrown out—like cookies whose shape didn't turn out quite right, or macs that were made by mistake—and instead of throwing them away, we put them in small cups and gave them out as free samples to people who were waiting for tables. Customers gobbled up the samples and were overjoyed when they would see a tray emerge from the kitchen. This made waiting an experience to look forward to rather than simply endure and fostered a celebratory vibe in the waiting area. The free samples had the side benefit of contributing to added dessert sales, as people tried things that they liked and were excited to order them later. This was all done with food that most restaurants would throw away, but we used it to help make waiting a special experience.

Making people feel seen and included was not just a practice, but had been baked into the design of the restaurant. At the time, I noticed that most restaurants fell into one of two categories: either fancy restaurants offering beautiful surroundings and impeccable service, or cheap restaurants that may offer great food but with shitty ambience and minimal service. I grew up eating superlative Thai food under fluorescent lighting in strip malls around Los Angeles, and tacos dished out of the window of food trucks on broken sidewalks. These restaurants offered incredible food, but were not the kind of places I sought out on a special occasion. Then there were restaurants like the ones I had worked for in New York—places with designer furniture and dim lighting and exposed brick walls, where fashionable servers floated from table to table delivering exquisite food and service. These places were great for an anniversary or a birthday, but not within reach for me or most people most of the time. When I thought about what I wanted to build at Homeroom, I believed that if I could bring the level of design and service that I had learned about in fancy restaurants to an approachable food like macaroni and cheese, I would create something truly special.

The thing is, great design and service don't need to cost more—they just require greater imagination. We couldn't afford expensive design services, so I scoured magazines and websites for fun ideas that would make the space feel special. We ended up making a chandelier out of cheap glass balls from Ikea. We built a living wall and filled it with plant clippings from all over the streets of Oakland. We created tables from old high school bleachers with little messages like "Lisa and James 4eva" still scraped into the surface. These little touches added up to make the space feel cozy and special, and ironically wound up being featured in multiple design blogs and websites.

I looked at every design element as an opportunity to invite customers to connect with the space. My favorite way we did this was through a repurposed card catalog I scavenged from the UC Berkeley Library. Before the digital age, physical cards would sit in a large wooden drawer with information about every book in the library, and finding a book would require flipping through them. UC Berkeley was getting rid of all of their card catalogs, and so I swooped in to grab one, along with thousands of cards. I created our customer loyalty program out of it, with space on each card for guests to put their name on a card, and keep it on file at the restaurant. They would get a gold star sticker for every mac ordered, and their tenth mac was free. Keeping their card at the restaurant instead of in their wallet made people feel like they were part of the space and had something to look forward to when they visited. It was an extra touch that cost nothing except a bit of my time and thought and delighted the hell out of people. Guests would decorate their cards to make them stand out in the drawers, and add character that made it their own. Whenever I was feeling low, I would go to the card catalog and flip through the cards, and invariably the cute notes and decorative artwork that people had left there brightened my mood.

Another invitation to engage was with our menu—it was designed to be turned into a paper airplane, so instead of handing the menu back like it was ours after ordering, customers would keep them and make the menus their own. After ordering, folks would fold up their menus, wind them up, and send them flying. Kids and adults alike would decorate their planes and take pride in them. Unfortunately, we had to change the design when one disgruntled customer was hit in the face by a paper airplane and nearly started a fight with another one—but it was fun while it lasted.

Something important about hospitality is that people can't give it unless they also get it. It was important to me that the thoughtfulness behind the design of the restaurant extended beyond the guests, and into spaces where staff worked. I had worked at many fancy restaurants that had beautiful spaces for customers to occupy, and then prison-like spaces for the staff to work. The next time you dine out, look to see if the kitchen in the restaurant has a window to the outside. Almost none do. Windows, and natural light, are generally reserved for customers. Architects and designers create dining rooms that monopolize all the natural light and street views for customers. The best chance that a chef usually has at natural light is if they work in an open kitchen, and even then, it's just the light that makes its way through the dining room, past the customers, and the leftovers seep into the kitchen. Having worked in such dreary spaces, I knew that I wanted staff to feel the same way that customers do—I wanted them to be able to look out the window and feel like they were part of the experience, the community, and the world around them when they are at work. If you've ever spent the day in a Las Vegas casino, you'll know that a world without natural sunlight is a great way to make your body lose all sense of time, place, and sanity. So, against all advice, we built the Homeroom kitchen next to windows that have the same view that customers have.

I couldn't have articulated it at the time, but I have come to understand that part of the secret sauce of building a great organization is a dedication to connection at all levels. Plenty of companies are famous for their connection to the customer, but far fewer take similar care with building such deep connections with their employees or community, or even creating workplaces where people can really connect with themselves. For example, Amazon's slogan is "The world's most customer-centric company," and they are well known for having impeccable customer service but being a difficult work environment. Many shitty jobs I held had that in common—a focus on treating the customer like royalty, but staff as disposable. In focusing only on the connection we can readily monetize, we miss all the other connections that matter in creating something more fulfilling, and I believe, ultimately more sustainably compelling.

In retrospect, creating the welcoming culture at Homeroom was just a replication of the system I was raised with—Jewish hospitality featuring American food. The tea and homemade cookies offered to visitors in my childhood morphed into tea and homemade cookies offered to the guests of Homeroom. The bond that this creates with complete strangers is the warm feeling that fueled my long days in the restaurant, and is the glue that brought people back again and again, even when we were fucking up left and right in those early days.

I even included a homemade Oreo (made with vegetable shortening instead of lard out of deference to vegetarians. . .sigh) on our opening menu as an homage to my parents' first meeting. Sampling it out to customers on the street reminded me of my parents, of the power of strangers coming together through food, and of the world of possibility that can be born from the simple act of sharing a cookie.

I couldn't have articulated it at the time, but I have come to understand that part of the secret sauce of building a great organization is a dedication to connection at all levels.

14

Training

Why the Best Instruction Resembles a Coloring Book

"When you know better, you do better."

—*Maya Angelou*

As the early months passed, Homeroom was like a ship caught in a storm, manned by a crew a quarter of the size of what was necessary to keep it afloat. There was a tight-knit group of die-hard loyalists at the core, like Dre and Ryan, running around like mad, trying to keep the ship from sinking. And then there was a rotating cast of characters that would come aboard, see that the ship was in severe distress, and decide they would rather just jump in the ocean.

My diary at the time:

February 16—Kitchen was a sweaty mess. Omar's girlfriend called in to say he was in the hospital an hour after we opened. I asked what hospital, so we could send flowers. No response. Need more staff. Much, much more staff.

February 18—Our line was over 100 people long and we took forever to cook everyone's meal. I found Tiffany crying again in the broom closet mid-shift. She says she is struggling to connect emotionally with our customers based on how we take orders. I don't think her tears are about the service model. Omar still MIA. I hope he is not dead.

February 19—Was up until 2 trying to figure out how to improve the hour-long wait for food. I am committed to making every single mac fresh to order, but it is taking forever. We are handing out as much free food as we are selling in an attempt to keep customers happy, but I don't know how long their patience will last. Martin quit. He said that cooking mac and cheese over and over is not the life of a chef he had dreamt of. Tiffany quit too. I think Omar is not coming back. Two people are taking vacation. I think this is what hell looks like.

February 20—Started having servers come in to grate cheese 4 hours before service because the kitchen is so short staffed. I am not sure how long we will keep servers that come in at the ass-crack of dawn to do kitchen work. Am trying to hire more, but not sure when that is supposed to happen when I am already working 18 hours a day.

February 21—Restaurant closed. Thank God. Slept for 16 hours.

February 22—Got voicemail from a customer that their credit card was stolen by a server. I didn't believe them, until they showed me security footage from Walgreens, where the customer's missing card resurfaced to purchase dozens of beauty products, clearly by the server. Confronted the server, and she denied it

109

was her, which caught me off-guard since it is very obviously her in the footage. I fired her, which I have never done before. It made me feel like throwing up. Staff of 14 down to 10.

February 23—Hired two new people—brothers. One, Josh, is super-fast on the line—like a little bolt of lightning running through the kitchen. So grateful.

March 6—I turned 30 two days ago. Friends came in from out of town, and I spent 24 hours asleep. Best birthday ever.

March 7—My friends Kristen and Tina came in for lunch today and said thanks for the comped meal. Except I didn't comp their meal. Turns out Darius did, in exchange for a killer tip. Turns out he is doing this to many, many tables. I am too tired to fire him, glad he resigned when I pointed it out. Staff down to 11. Even the host is here at 5 am to grate cheese.

March 8—Josh got caught doing cocaine in the alleyway during break. Am embarrassed that I thought maybe he was just really exuberant about cooking mac and cheese every day. Staff down to 10 again.

It turns out that a business with no rules is just as shitty and dysfunctional as a business with a lot of rules—the dysfunction just has a different flair. Even though we were struggling with big things like attendance and drug abuse, it became clear to me that these issues were just a natural outgrowth of the lack of structure much further upstream. Sort of like telling a kid in a candy store that they should regulate their own candy intake—don't be surprised when you come back and the place is cleaned out.

Staff complained of stress in preparing for work—was this skirt too short? Was it okay to wear a hoodie over their head? Even though there were not rules, we all know there *were* rules—they were just unstated, which is the very worst kind. Staff knew that it would not be acceptable to wear something like, say, a bikini to work, and yet, without me expressing where the line was, they were left to guess. And there is nothing as fun as getting ready in the morning and guessing whether your boss is going to approve of your T-shirt choice.

Although the dress code was a source of stress and confusion, it was the vacation policy that really put the *fun* in dysfunction. While today many tech companies have adopted a similar vacation policy, a restaurant is not like a software company. If Jenny the programmer wants to take an extra day off, there is probably someone one desk over who can cover for her. Or maybe whatever new program she was working on can just sit calmly on her desk, awaiting her return. In a restaurant, if Jenny the server wants a day off, there needs to be an extra person, not already working, to be there. Customers can't just be put down for a day—they are going to show up, and they need people to cook their food and clean their tables. And it turns out that when people are chronically overworked in a restaurant that is chronically understaffed, they need vacation. A lot of vacation.

What I had missed was that in my reactivity to top-down traditional rules, I had just replaced one kind of top-down rule structure with another one. Instead of traditional rules like uniforms and strict vacation policies, I had just unilaterally instituted nontraditional rules that did away with them but that still came from above with no input from anyone else. I was so focused on being different and creating the kind of culture that I wanted that I created the kind of culture that no one wanted.

I knew I needed to build something different but was stuck on how to do it. Weeks and months passed like a blur, until one night a 30-something-year-old man came in with his parents for dinner. His wife had recently given birth to a baby that was premature and required a lengthy hospital stay, so she was still in the hospital while he and his parents were out for a quick bite, some fresh air, and to bring his wife back some dinner. Ryan corralled both servers and kitchen folks to surround the table with a caramel brownie sundae with a huge candle in it, and sang a rousing happy birthday to the new baby. We filmed it, so the new father could share the celebration with his wife, then sent her a free mac and cheese to congratulate her. Ryan wrapped up a Homeroom onesie for the baby with a gift card for her first mac when she was older, and tucked in a little card welcoming her to the world that was signed by everyone on staff that night. The new father broke into tears before he left.

These kinds of interactions are what kept us all going (and thankfully, what kept our guests returning despite our chaotic disorganization at the time), and I asked Ryan what had given him this idea.

"I try to stoke out at least five tables per shift," Ryan responded, matter-of-factly. "It's like, my personal goal."

"How did you come up with that?" I asked.

What I had missed was that in my reactivity to top-down traditional rules, I had just replaced one kind of top-down rule structure with another one.

"We serve so many people every day," Ryan said, "and I got a little overwhelmed trying to do something super-special for all of them. So I decided that while I would obviously try my best with everyone, I would focus on picking out five tables—like one every hour or two—where I would do something really, really big."

"That's amazing," I said.

"Yeah," Ryan responded, "it's been really fun. That guy was one of my stoke-out guests today—it seemed like he needed it."

Around that time, I had been struggling to put together service standards for the new staff we kept hiring (then losing). I knew that people needed some kind of guidance and training on how to be a good server, and my brand of "I trust you" was not cutting it. At the same time, I didn't like that most restaurants handle this problem by using scripts that feel inauthentic, and that make people feel like human robots that can't be trusted to use their brains. Many restaurants have specific customer service scripts for everything from how to greet a table to reinforce brand loyalty ("Welcome to Applebee's!") or take an order to encourage upselling ("Would you like fries with that?"). That felt decidedly yucky to me.

What I loved about what Ryan had come up with is that it provided structure to his service—stoke out at least five tables every shift—but then within that boundary gave him complete freedom and creativity to express himself. The way that Ryan would stoke out that new father would probably look completely different from how someone else might. Since I had been taking a crash course in what a freak-show complete freedom at work looks like, this idea of freedom within prescribed boundaries of an expectation seemed like a logical evolution.

Over many late-night chats with a small, tight-knit core of Ryan, Dre, and Mick, we would spitball ideas on how to improve service and make the staff experience more enjoyable. I loved these chats, and through them I started to see the outlines of the kind of a middle path that was uniquely Homeroom. To replace the dreaded uniform policy, we collaborated on a structure of basic rules for safety and kindness (i.e. no shirts with offensive language), and then gave people freedom within that to express themselves and wear what they wanted. It turns out that having a clear boundary actually made people feel freer to experiment within it, and servers would comment enthusiastically on how much they loved it. I would find that over and over the key to making people feel free wasn't complete freedom as I had imagined—it was figuring out where the boundary line should be and offering freedom of expression within that space.

I could never have dreamt up the stoke-out rule, but it became a cornerstone of our service model and an example of how to do things the Homeroom way. There was structure and expectation surrounding how to serve customers, but how staff decided to do so was completely their own, and they were given total freedom within that constraint to decide what would be meaningful to them and whatever guests they were connecting with. I saw staff write poems on napkins, draw cartoons on take-out bags, create an off-menu mac and cheese and name it after a guest, spell out "prom" in peas atop a mac to help a high schooler ask his crush to prom. The collective imagination of staff working within the boundary of the stoke-out rule created moving experiences on a regular basis and made it fun to come to work. Establishing common boundaries with my team created a safe container for people to express themselves genuinely and connect in ways that a strict rule or script would never have supported.

Many years in, I ultimately realized that my greatest role as a leader was just to work on *collaborative container creation*—on everything from how to run a meeting to how to fix a mistake. Working with everyone who was an expert—my staff—to figure out how to build the structures that maximally support people being themselves at work, while still functioning as a team, is an art we stumbled through and practiced on the daily.

I would find that over and over the key to making people feel free wasn't complete freedom as I had imagined—it was figuring out where the boundary line should be and offering freedom of expression within that space.

An image I would return to again and again is a coloring book. My young son, Isaac, never really enjoyed art—there was something overwhelming about a big, empty page that he didn't know what to do with. But when I gave him a coloring book filled with images to be brought to life, he was obsessed. All of a sudden, he knew what he was making, and could make it his own by filling it in with color.

My job was to hand our staff not a blank piece of paper but a coloring book—people wanted to know what the hell they were doing, but within that wanted to express their creativity. By contrast, most places I had worked doled out paint-by-numbers, where you are told exactly what to do and there was no room for personal creativity or expression. Everyone's paint-by-number will look the same, but not everyone's coloring book. And everyone's blank page will look super-different, but in my experience this leads to abject chaos. So if you are trying to figure out how to do this where you work, when creating expectations for employees, ask yourself if you are handing someone a blank page, a paint-by-number, or a coloring book. The answer will define how things are done, how much creativity is valued, and how much fun everyone will have while doing it.

15

Culture

The Centerpiece of Great Workplaces and Dairy Products

"I would rather walk with a friend in the dark than alone in the light."
—*Helen Keller*

Much controversy surrounds the mythology of how I met one of my best friends, Nina. The facts that everyone can agree upon are that we were both about one year old, and that there was a park involved, but after that the stories diverge widely.

According to my mother (who, admittedly, was not there, but that never stops her from asserting that she alone knows the truth), I was playing in the sandbox, when I spotted Nina from the corner of my eye. We made eye contact, and like a meet-cute moment for the toddler set, immediately waddled toward each other and embraced. We began playing with each other, and when my father and her mother noticed our natural affinity for each other, they began chatting and exchanged phone numbers so they could get us together.

According to Nina's mother, Sarina, there was no sandbox involved. Sarina was walking home from the park with Nina in a stroller when my father passed her in his car and pulled over. He rolled down the window, and as she braced for some form of harassment, he shouted from the car window.

"Hey—my wife just had a baby, too. How old is your little one?"

"Um," Sarina stammered, unsure of what to make of a strange man pulling over to talk to her, "She's one."

"That's wonderful," said my dad, "My daughter Erin is one, too. Perhaps we can get them together sometime?"

My father wrote down his phone number on a piece of paper from his glove box and handed it to her. "My wife's name is Helen, and I'm Al. We hope to hear from you." And with that, he drove off.

Two days later, Sarina called to arrange a playdate.

Whether from a creepy drive-by pickup job by my dad or a moment of profound love in a sandbox between Nina and me, we'll never know what began our friendship.

To me, the act of friendship is synonymous with creating a chosen family. It is a lifelong bond that is a foundation to return to over time, distance, break-ups, heartache, career shifts, and personal growth.

What we do know is that even though our parents were never friends and we never attended the same schools, Nina and I were inseparable throughout our childhood.

We were elementary-school adventurers who jumped off the balcony at her dad's apartment using homemade parachutes (aka sheets) to see if we could fly (we could not, and yes, that landing hurt like a motherfucker). We were teenagers rolling around in her dad's vintage Mustang convertible as he screamed at Nina from the passenger's seat, "You're going to kill us!" We were 20-somethings who spent Thanksgiving together in a crowded apartment without a functioning oven, eating vegan stuffed mushrooms while researching how to cook a turkey in a fireplace. We were 30-somethings who had daughters within a year of each other, girls who would never attend the same school or even live in the same city, but whom we got together frequently and hoped would become great friends as we had.

To me, the act of friendship is synonymous with creating a chosen family. It is a lifelong bond that is a foundation to return to over time, distance, breakups, heartache, career shifts, and personal growth. It ebbs and it flows. Some moments are closer than others, but it is always there in the background, ready to support, love, or just have a damn good time.

During my lawyer days, when people would talk about having friends at work, I would nod my head like I understood what they were talking about while secretly feeling like a complete misanthrope. I viewed work and fun as two separate categories, and spending time in one meant having less time for the other. In my mind, the only thing worse than being with my coworkers on weekdays was being with them on weekends. But something about starting my own company and doing work with my whole heart made me want to show up in a fuller way. I didn't want to have a work life and a personal life that needed to be separated—I wanted to just have a life that could be lived fully everywhere.

As the months after opening stretched into years, press began taking notice of our upstart mac and cheese operation. Legitimate news outlets took a shine to us—we were featured on the Cooking Channel and written up in the *Wall Street Journal*. Even Guy Fieri's *Diners, Drive-ins, and Dives* contacted us about featuring us, then backed out because we had already become too famous (apparently Guy only covers restaurants that he alone has "discovered").

Our staff was generally proud to work for us, and those who didn't steal credit cards or have nervous breakdowns from stress had become like family. Even after a long week at work, we all played on a soccer team together during the one day a week the restaurant was closed. Those who didn't like to play often came to cheer from the sidelines holding up homemade signs, hauling out coolers with snacks and beer for everyone to enjoy afterwards.

The sense of camaraderie that is built when everyone is truly working together is profound. People from other professions would feel the spirit of the place, and ask if they could come and work with us. A friend of mine from law school, a hard-ass, tattooed prosecutor named Bone, asked to moonlight on weekends. By day she had to cover up all her tattoos under a suit to look professional, but at nights with us she would put on a sleeveless shirt and let her hair down. Bone would high-five people who had suffered a long wait when they finally got to a table, crack jokes with people in line, hand out hunks of chalk, and offer up prizes for the best sidewalk art. Bone was a six-figure-salary professional who chose to spend her weekends working with us for a fraction of her normal hourly pay because of how good it felt to be part of something.

Our customers could also feel the genuine affection and care among the staff, and it lent a warmth to the space that was palpable. We felt bonded by the common purpose of doing a hard thing together—making a new restaurant a reality, functioning just a little bit better day by day. Over time, though, I began to understand that the pitfalls of work family are very similar to the pitfalls of regular family.

For one, family will hit you up for favors. I had employees ask for personal loans and advances on paychecks. It was hard to say no when someone had car troubles or needed a security deposit to afford a new apartment. But there wasn't just one or two requests like this—I got them all the time. Restaurant work is low wage and everyone is living on the margins, so these kinds of asks came in regularly and I started to feel like some kind of Las Vegas bookie trying to keep track of what people owed me. As our staff swelled, I began to realize that this kind of interdependence was unsustainable and creating considerable stress. I was afraid that someone might not pay me back, and that certain people were more reliable than others but that if I was willing to give advances or loans to some people, I had to be willing to do it for all.

Another problem with family is that you can't fire them. When someone was underperforming, it felt too emotionally painful to let them go. So instead, I would do with my work family what I did with my regular family—which is to point out what I wanted to be different and then lose my mind with frustration when it would not change.

The last problem I ran into was an extension of the one above—because we all felt so close, I felt abandoned when people left. Yes, sometimes people need to move or start school, but when someone would leave for another job I was devastated. Coming to work at Homeroom was like meeting Nina in the sandbox—it was meant to be a moment that would foster years of connection and growth. I thought my coworkers and I were building something that was forever.

I came to a turning point on the issue one day over ice cream. A lot of ice cream. I was visiting a mentor—the founder of Amy's Ice Cream in Austin, Texas—and chatting with their head of training, a bubbly force of nature named Kara.

"Kara," I said, between bites of a rum-soaked flavor, Bahama Mama, "This place is incredible. I love that you have such a beautiful training room and someone entirely dedicated to education. Do people never want to leave here?"

"Of course not," she replied, "I mean, we're an ice cream shop. People leave all the time."

"Huh," I said. "Does that bug you?"

"Not really," she replied. "It's part of our model, really. We know that scooping ice cream is going to be most people's first job, not their last job. This is the kind of thing people do while they're in school, or heading to somewhere else. We know we're going to be a stopover on most people's professional journey, so our goal is to be a memorable part of their life. Like, we want them to think of Amy's fondly, to be glowing alumni who want to gush to friends about us, and to talk about their time at Amy's as not just one of their favorite work experiences, but as one of their favorite life experiences. That feels really meaningful to us, and it's a big part of how we have built a loyal, long-term fan base."

As I soaked in Kara's message, I felt myself begin breathing a little more freely. An almost tangible sensation of relief trickled down into my chest when I realized that there was a different way to achieve the outcome I was after. I loved that walking into Amy's was like walking into Homeroom—I could feel the warmth of the staff right there on the surface. It had not occurred to me that I could build this kind of connectivity with a very different philosophy than the one I was using.

When I returned home, I thought for a long time about what kind of philosophy I wanted to guide my working relationships. I had been completely dismissive of them while I was a lawyer, which felt like shit. But now I had swung the pendulum as far as possible in the other direction and made my coworker community like a second, dysfunctional family. This also felt like shit. I needed a different paradigm.

I started reading all sorts of nerdy books about different kinds of leadership models. I read about *holocracy*, a system where people pick their own job titles and meet in circles every week to decide how to run things together. Holocracy seemed like a patchouli-inflected hippie-fest, like if you turned 1960s counterculture Berkeley into a model for corporate governance. It seemed interesting until I began learning about its most famous proponent, Tony Hsieh, the eccentric leader of Zappos who died tragically in a drug-addled cabal in a burning shed. His experiment with holocracy at Zappos resulted in nearly 20 percent of his workforce quitting and years later was decried as a failure. The company returned to a more traditional model. The main problem: it turns out that people like understanding what their job is and what they are supposed to do at work instead of having to invent it themselves. Asking restaurant workers to define their own roles in the midst of cooking and delivering mac and cheese seemed like the premise for a compelling game show, but a terrible business model. I would have to keep looking.

One night I was rocking my infant daughter to sleep and singing to her in my signature off-key voice. Her eyes were closing, and I felt myself ready to nod off alongside her. The Homeroom team had a soccer game, and there was nothing I felt like doing less than playing at what should have been my bedtime after a long day of working and momming. Reluctantly, I tucked her into her crib, threw my cleats into a duffel bag, and headed toward the field.

When I arrived, folks were on the sidelines stretching and jogging the length of the field to warm up. We circled up as the game began to give ourselves a cheer in a giant huddle, and erupted in laughter as we all tried to high five. At kick-off, Diego was making a run toward the goal when he was taken out of the game by an opponent's cleat to his knee. Another cook, Remy, ran in to replace him, but at two decades older he was struggling to keep up with the pace of the game. We all cheered Remy on as he did his best to hustle and moved him into another position at halftime that required less movement on the field.

As I watched Remy stagger into his new position and a fresher player take over his role, something clicked. I was struggling so much at work to do something that was so easy on that field—moving a player into a role because of their performance, and adjusting who gets to play based on nothing more than the best players and combinations to win the game. It was not hard to pull out Diego when he was couldn't play well or to move Remy to a different role because it suited his skills better. At work, however, I was struggling to let go of people who were no longer pulling their weight because I felt beholden to them. But just like leaving a limping Diego on the field would have dragged down the entire team, so was letting lower-performance employees stay on at Homeroom.

A few days later was a weekly leadership meeting we called recess. My leadership team at the time consisted of six 30-somethings with about 80 tattoos between them. There was a preponderance of skateboarding skill among them, but scant restaurant experience. One was named after a vegetable, while another went by the Spanish nickname for sandal. It was the first time in leadership positions for all of us.

"Okay everyone, gather round," I called out. When the group was assembled, I continued, "I've been thinking about this for a while, and I wanted to talk about how we all work together."

Everyone perked up, and sat up a little straighter.

"I am so proud of the Homeroom family we have built, but am realizing that as we grow bigger, it is fucking hard to be like a family. Thinking of ourselves in this way has allowed us to be incredibly close but to run Homeroom in a way that is not giving us the best chance at success."

Everyone looked a bit apprehensive. Their nervousness caused me to increase my cadence, hoping if I could get through what I had to say, our nerves would be calmed.

"We are almost 50 people strong, and growing larger each day. When I look to the future, what I see is that we need to evolve into a team, and not a family. I want us to be the best team—one that adores each other and plays beautifully together. On a team, there is accountability—everyone has a role to play, and if they aren't pulling their weight, then we need to send in someone else who can. On a team, some players are core and will remain for years, while others will rotate onto other teams, retire,

You can't create something new without having to let go of something old.

or move on. Teammates are always learning from each other and always learning to adapt to new configurations with new players."

The group was quiet, taking it in.

"I have also been reflecting on my own role. Currently, I'm out there playing alongside you—running dishes on busy nights, helping take orders—while also being your coach—leading meetings, figuring out strategy. My years as a player helped me figure out how to be a better coach, but it's time for me to really dig into my role as coach and not try to juggle playing at the same time. I want to dedicate myself to figuring out how to make us the best team we can be."

"So how do we do that?" asked Dre.

"I have no idea," I said.

Tension hung in the air at that meeting. Change is always a bit scary. You can't create something new without having to let go of something old. For me, letting go of that old thing also came with a twinge of sadness. I thought warmly of my childhood adventures with Nina, and how those moments garnered some of the same warm feelings I had experienced during my best moments with my staff. It was time for the wild ride that was the startup experience of Homeroom to mature, and I realized that not all the people who had started with us would readily make it to the next phase. It was not like Nina and me on the playground—we were doing something altogether different at Homeroom. And while it still involved the same larger-than-life amounts of mac and cheese as my childhood, it was time for us to evolve from chosen family into a team.

16 | Discipline

On Spanking, Cages, and All the Weird Ways We Punish People

"If you're going to do something wrong, do it big, because the punishment is the same either way."

—*Jayne Mansfield*

I grew up in the '80s, when spanking was a thing. I'm not talking about the kinky sexual kind—I'm talking the Catholic nun in the little red school-house kind (although, now that I'm writing that, it sounds a bit kinky too). The flavor of spanking I grew up with was a swift slap on the ass when I was out of line. Hand in the cookie jar when it shouldn't be? Slap across the ass. You threw your brother's homework in the garbage can? Slap across the ass. Today this is categorized as child abuse, but at the time it was just thought of as firm parenting.

While I was a well-behaved kid who wasn't spanked very often, I do recall the last time it happened. I don't remember what I did wrong, but I do remember the anger welling up inside me when my dad hit me. A blinding heat behind my eyes bubbled over, and I started punching my dad in his middle-aged man-gut. I couldn't have been older than nine, but I unleashed my fists of fury all over his 220-pound frame. I remember the perplexed look on his face at this reversal of aggression. If he hit me back, we would actually be in a fist fight, and I could see him calculating that this was not an accept-able outcome. He grabbed my wrists, telling me to stop, and then slunk away down the hallway to his bedroom. He never hit me again.

Punishment is a funny thing. It's in the air that we breathe, so we don't stop to think about just how warped some of the messaging is. My dad is a sweet, gentle man, but the lesson of spanking was that if I didn't follow his rules, he would physically hurt me.

It's not really different as we age—the messaging just becomes institu-tionalized. When I was in junior high, I was caught passing notes in class and got detention. The message there was that if I didn't follow the rules of my school (presumably there to facilitate learning), I would be forced into more not-learning. I had to sit in a room with a teacher paid to ensure that I stared blankly at the wall and did *not* learn for an hour. I am not sure why they would punish a student who wasn't learning by forcing her not to learn even more (and then add insult to injury by making a teacher sit there and not teach), but there it is.

When I was older and worked as a lawyer, I found it odd that we do similar things to adults. Did you steal a candy bar from the grocery store? Well then, we're going to put you in a cage. Get caught with drugs? You're going in the cage. Evade your taxes? Cage. There is something awfully weird about putting people in cages for doing something wrong.

I worked in a prosecutor's office all through law school—not because I believed in putting people in cages, but because I thought that something had to change, and that I'd be in a better position to do something about it in a position of power. It turns out that people put in cages aren't all that different from me as a nine-year-old, pummeling my dad. When they get out, they are not focused on their own wrongdoing, but filled with anger at the system that put them there.

Becoming a boss at Homeroom for the first time meant I had to decide how I wanted to approach the issue of punishment. The only system that I had seen modeled was the draconian one I grew up with. In restaurants I had worked at, if I was late for a shift, I would receive a write-up or be sent home. Punished for showing up late to work by having me not work even more. The whole thing seemed a lot like detention, and just made me feel like a victim, ready to unleash my fists of fury at my boss instead of looking inside and contemplating what I had done wrong.

When you work in a restaurant, every day presents an opportunity to interact with deviant behavior. Because restaurants are entertainment, they are busiest when the normal world is just winding down. A job that requires working nights, weekends, and holidays doesn't exactly attract those called to a life of stability. Homeroom is a family-friendly restaurant, but the dinner staff still routinely leave at midnight. We begin our wind-down over drinks at 1 a.m., and get in bed when the rest of the world is waking up. No one is going home to have dinner with their spouse, put their kids to bed, or spend Memorial Day at the backyard BBQ. Add the fact that entry-level restaurant work is minimum wage labor, and you'll notice that your labor pool is unfairly stacked with young folks trying their hand at working for the first time, people hiding addiction issues in plain sight, and a whole lot of hard-working immigrants juggling multiple jobs.

I'll never forget when one of my favorite employees, a server who had worked with me for years, called me a year after she had left Homeroom. She was in AA, working the steps, and called to apologize for how she had left the job with little notice. She had been struggling with alcoholism for years, and had been in a particularly dark place when she left. She had also been one of my highest-performing employees, and I'd had no clue. It made me wonder what was going on with everyone else.

What I found about people who do deviant shit at work is that they fall into two categories: those who don't know what they are supposed to do and those who do. Let's start with the first group, because a shocking number of people fall into that category. Global research by Gallup found that only about half of employees know what is expected of them at work.[1] Half! That is a lot of people making excuses to visit the snack bin and lingering over their phones in bathroom stalls worldwide.

I worked with a statuesque cashier, Fabio, in my early days at Homeroom. His job was to enter take-out orders into the system and help customers with anything from beer selection to walking take-out boxes to their car. On a slow lunch shift, I passed him sitting behind the counter and reading a book. He looked up, flashed me a smile, and went back to reading his book. I was livid. Who the hell did this guy think he was, being paid to read on the job? My mind went to all kinds of uncharitable places, including that his good looks had let him get away with all sorts of shitty behavior his entire life. By the time I opened my mouth to say something, I had projected all my middle-school pretty-people resentment on this poor 20-something, and I was ready to make the world a better place by firing him.

"Hey Fabio," I said briskly, "What are you doing?"

"I am reading this really good book from my philosophy class. It's called. . ."

"Um," I interrupted, "I don't care what it's called. I'm wondering why you're reading it here, at work?"

His body language shifted. He stood up from his stool, and took a small step back from me.

"Oh, well, uh, I guess it's because there was nothing else to do. It's pretty slow and I finished all the prep work for the shift, and there's no customers here right now."

I paused. My mind started racing. Did this guy honestly think it was okay to read at work? Fuck. I think he does think this is okay. How could anyone possibly think that? Except, I think he actually does think that. Fuck.

"Okay," I blurted out after an uncomfortably long pause. "There's a saying in restaurants—'time to lean, time to clean.' So whenever you think

---

[1] Marco Nink, "Many Employees Don't Know What's Expected of Them at Work," Gallup, October 13, 2015, https://news.gallup.com/businessjournal/186164/employees-don-know-expected-work.aspx.

you're done with everything you're expected to do, find something to clean. Dust the shelves, deep-clean the beer fridge, mop the floor. No more books on shift—you understand?"

"Yes," he stammered. "Um, yes, totally. Sorry about that."

He put his book on a shelf under the register, grabbed a rag, and started wiping down the counters.

I feel bad saying it out loud, but I had honestly thought that Fabio was lazy, dumb, or both. He was none of the above—he just didn't understand what was expected of him. Fabio ended up having an incredible work ethic, and I never saw him on his heels again. I was genuinely sad when he moved away and left the team.

The funny thing I found about people who don't know what they are supposed to do at work is that I started off blaming them but ultimately realized that I was actually the person at fault. I would make all sorts of assumptions about what people should know how to do, but I'm not sure how I thought they were supposed to magically know all these things. It should not be on the shoulders of a new employee to know something important without it being communicated. So we started devoting a few minutes of our new hire orientation to saying the "time to lean, time to clean" mantra out loud, and didn't have an experience like Fabio again.

But what do you do if someone does know that they did something wrong, and did it anyway? This is the far thornier issue.

Let's be real here for a minute. I have absolutely been that asshole who has feigned illness to miss work, made up a reason for why I couldn't possibly get a project done on time, or lied through my teeth about why I was late. All of sudden, though, I was the boss of a legion of people just like me, and struggling like hell to figure out what to do about it.

For a while, I tried all the stuff that had been tried on me at other jobs because I hadn't really had anything else modeled and didn't know what else to do. During a particularly dark moment when I was having trouble getting people to show up on time to shifts, I instituted a three-strikes policy. If someone was late three times, they would be fired.

You know who else instituted a three-strikes policy? California's prison system. In the '90s, in response to an explosion in violent crime, California voters decided to impose life imprisonment on anyone who committed three violent offenses. The measure has been widely viewed as a failure—it takes some violent criminals off the streets forever, but our society produces a steady stream of new ones, so it didn't achieve its objective of reducing violent crime. Similarly, I could get rid of employees who were routinely breaking the rules, but it generally meant firing fully trained people who broke rules only to let in completely untrained people who broke rules to replace them.

An even bigger problem was that some of our best employees broke these rules all the time. When one of our strongest servers, Dave, was late for his third shift, I realized I was in a pickle. This guy was beloved by customers—people would routinely ask to be seated in his section because he was so damn delightful, and fellow staff members nominated him for employee awards because he would always help them on shift and went above and beyond on cleaning and side work. He would often pick up other people's duties just to make their day. There was no way in hell I was going to fire this guy, but if I didn't follow the rule, I would lose all my legitimacy. We had to change it.

I thought back to a philosophy I had learned about in law school called restorative justice. The theory behind it is that instead of punishing people for wrongdoing, the goal should be to get as close as possible to righting a wrong. For example, if someone steals a necklace, traditional justice would send them to jail but restorative justice would have them give it back to the original owner, acknowledge the harm they had caused, and do whatever possible to make the victim feel safe again.

I began to wonder what it would look like to get people to right their wrongs instead of punishing them. The problem was, I couldn't figure out how someone who was chronically late could correct for their mistake other than by always being on time. Wasn't that what I was giving them the opportunity to do with my three-strikes rule? I started poring through books and articles on restorative justice, but I could not figure out how to handle something as silly as someone being late. How can someone possibly make that right?

So I decided to do what I often did when I had no clue how to proceed—just try it. I read a bit about the structure of restorative conversations and decided to wing it with Dave. I went through some basics with his manager, Dre, and called the two in to give this thing a whirl.

"Hey folks," I said, "take a seat." I had cleared a table in the empty dining room and placed three seats around it in a circle.

They sat down gingerly, Dre staring straight at me and Dave looking down at the floor.

"I wanna try something here today, and I'm honestly not sure how it's going to go, but my intention is to strengthen our trust in each other and make Homeroom a better place to work. How does that sound?"

"I'm really sorry," Dave blurted out, his knee bouncing up and down, "I know why we're here—I'm always late. It's been a problem my whole life—I'm just not great at watching the time. I totally understand if you want to let me go. I'm really, really sorry . . . ."

"I'm not here to fire you," I interrupted. "But I appreciate you recognizing that you being chronically late is why we're here." (Step one in restorative conversation: What happened? Check!) "I'm actually hoping that we could start by talking about the impact of you being late." (Step two in restorative conversation: What is the impact? Double check!)

"Well," Dave said, "other staff get stretched thin trying to cover my tables."

"That's true," I replied, then paused to see if there was more.

Dave looked blankly at me.

Dre shifted in her seat and spoke up, "What is it like when you work a short-staffed shift?"

"It sucks," Dave said. "The whole place just feels angry and anxious. Customers get annoyed because it takes them a long time to put in their order and get their food, and servers are really stressed out trying to juggle the needs of too many tables."

"So customers get bad service, and other staff members are really stressed out," Dre summarized.

"Yep," Dave said. "I guess it's also expensive for the restaurant. Like, paying overtime to whoever is staying on."

"True," said Dre. I nodded in agreement, though I embarrassingly had not even calculated that as one of the additional costs of people being late.

"So Dave," I asked, "what do you think it would take to make it right?" (Step three in restorative conversation: Making it right.)

At this question, Dave completely perked up. He adjusted himself and sat up a little taller in his chair. He started out slowly, but then his words spilled out faster and faster as he picked up steam.

"I mean, I could apologize to the staff. Maybe I can buy them a beer after work to say sorry. I could also get right in there and help. Like, maybe lighten other people's load by picking up their side work or their end-of-shift cleaning duties. I could offer to cover for them if there are days they are going on vacation or need coverage to help make it up to them."

He took a moment to catch his breath, then kept going.

"I could go to my tables to apologize for any interruptions in service and let them know it's because I was late. I could offer them a free dessert as an apology. You could dock my pay for those free desserts."

"That's not necessary, Dave," I added, "or legal, I don't think—but I appreciate the gesture."

"More than anything, I'll really try to get better at this," Dave said. "I get why this sucks for so many people, and I'm sorry."

"Thanks, Dave," I said, "I really appreciate the apology, but more than that, all your great ideas that would be so appreciated by other people if you're late again."

"Thanks," he said, looking me straight in the eye.

The conversation took all of ten minutes—less time than most people usually spend giving us excuses for being late, and significantly less time than it would have taken to draft a disciplinary write-up. More importantly, I loved that Dave had come up with so many meaningful ways to address the problems he had created—to diminish stress for staff on shift and improve bad service to customers. He was even aware of the ways his mistake was costing the company money, and I had to hand it to him for wanting to right that wrong as well.

I felt—dare I say it—strong! I was so used to feeling like a nagging parent about disciplinary issues that it felt empowering to hold space for someone else to figure out how to fix their own problems. Instead of me carrying the burden, it shifted the burden to Dave to fix it, and my only job was to ask the right questions and listen. Hell—he even came up with better ideas than I ever would have (we know this, because I had previously been using that damned three-strikes rule that wasn't making absolutely anything right).

Not every restorative conversation went as smoothly or as beautifully as the one with Dave. Some people shut down when confronted with their behavior, and others turned into defensive assholes. Many are incapable of getting outside themselves to see how they have impacted others, no matter how generously coached. But overall, once we started using restorative conversations to address crappy behavior, we witnessed a sea change not just in behavior, but in the depth of our connections with each other. It wasn't about cat and mouse, or parent and child—the dynamic was one of shared responsibility for something bigger than us. It was about maintaining positive relationships with each other and how well we were serving our community.

When we were focused on punishment, the question of whether to fire someone was about whether they had broken the rules. Once we shifted to a restorative lens, the question was whether or not someone was committed to building the kind of community we all wanted to live in. Instead of "Are they late?" we would ask, "Do they care about respecting other people's time, building trust, and creating a great experience for our community?"

Once we started thinking through that lens, it was also easier to let go of high-performance jerks. Like, in our early days when we were desperately understaffed, I had a tolerance for cooks who could bang out dishes faster than anyone but occasionally did so while treating others with disdain or a sense of entitlement. There was this one guy, Tim, who would routinely lose his temper when he got stressed out. His face would turn comically red, and he would start banging pots down on burners while he muttered expletives under his breath. Technically he wasn't breaking any rules, but spiritually he sucked up all the air in the room and made the kitchen feel like it was at the center of a stress ball in his vice grip.

When Tim was unable to control his temper after multiple restorative conversations, he decided to leave. Not because he had done something wrong per se, but because it became clear to him through our conversations that he was not going to be able to contribute to the kind of culture we were trying to build. Tim went on to work in a more traditional, Gordon Ramsay–style kitchen where his flare-ups were considered a normal byproduct of the job. But I was grateful that instead of having to hold Tim accountable for a different standard and firing him for not meeting it, he basically fired himself when the expectations of the culture became strong enough for him to realize he didn't belong anymore.

> *The dynamic was one of shared responsibility for something bigger than us. It was about maintaining positive relationships with each other and how well we were serving our community.*

The outcome of a tough situation is often less important than the process it takes to get there. And the beauty of this restorative process was that even if it ended in someone leaving, the conversations it took to get there left them feeling seen and heard in a way that traditional discipline did not. I ran into Tim a few months later at a new restaurant where he was working. He was hard at work on the line, but found a moment to send me out a free appetizer. I looked up to make eye contact with him, smiled, and mouthed, "Thank you." "Thank you," he mouthed back, and turned his head back down to the dish he was working on.

17 | Goals

Not Just for Motivational Posters

> "If you don't know where you're going, you'll end up someplace else."
> —*Yogi Berra*

At 18, a good friend of mine left home to attend college with legions of bright-eyed American teenagers. He had done well enough in high school to get into an Ivy League university, and his parents sent him off proudly with all the accoutrements of an upper-middle-class collegiate experience: fresh flannel sheets for his extra-long dorm bed, a spiffy new computer, and a checkbook linked to a personal bank account to help cover his expenses.

Halfway through the semester, he wrote a check and it bounced. He called his parents in a panic.

"Hi Mom," he said, "I think there's something wrong with my bank account."

"What is it, sweetie?" she responded.

"I wrote a check and it bounced. But I still have like ten more checks in the checkbook."

"Excuse me?" she asked.

"I still have ten checks left. So there should still be money left in there."

Silence.

"Mom?"

More silence.

"Honey, your account running out of money has nothing to do with how many checks you have left. If you wrote checks for more money than you have in your account, they won't go through. The account is not an endless supply of money limited only by how many checks you have. What if you wrote a check for a million dollars? If you don't have a million dollars in there, which you don't, the check won't clear."

More silence.

"Oh," he finally said.

Now in his 40s, my friend has never lived this story down. And while some might write his behavior off to privilege (fair), I am struck by his glaring lack of financial literacy in spite of his privilege. Here is a guy who was driven, smart, and fortunate enough to get into an Ivy League school, and yet even with some of the best American primary education under his belt, he didn't even know how a bank account works. He could do quantum physics but believed that checks had the power to make money appear like a magician at a five-year-old's birthday party.

You might be wondering what financial literacy has to do with, well, anything, but it turns out it has a lot to do with everything.

As I started to question how to turn my dysfunctional family at Homeroom into a team, I tried to break down what different kinds of teams had in common. I started thinking about my favorite teams. The LA Lakers of my 1980s youth. The US National Women's Soccer Team. Charlie's Angels. The X-Men. Whether playing a sport or fighting bad guys, the thing they have in common is kicking ass. Winning. Charlie's Angels and the X-Men wouldn't be awesome if they never caught the bad guy. The Lakers and the US Women's Soccer Team wouldn't be amazing if they didn't win all the time. But what the hell does it mean to win at running a business?

I started to get overwhelmed by what seemed to be our goals. Was it to make money? Sure—we couldn't really do anything else if we weren't making money. But our goal wasn't *just* to make money. What made Homeroom genuinely special was our ability to delight people—to be the best part of their day. To have customers dig into the best mac and cheese of their life, close their eyes, and lose themselves for a minute. How do we win at that? Also, even if we could make money and make the most delicious mac and cheese on the planet, if our staff were miserable, would we feel like we were winning? I don't think so. Employee happiness matters, too. So do we have to pick one thing that means winning? Can all of these things mean winning?

I started reading a lot of business books, a genre featuring more white men than a gun show in Idaho. The subject of most of these books seemed to be size. Specifically, how to grow larger. Some offered retrospectives on how some of America's biggest companies got so big. Others broke down the kinds of company cultures that support growth. Others offered leadership advice to help businesses (you guessed it) grow bigger. This theme felt like a grown-up version of comparing dick size, and like a game I was uninterested in playing.

This obsession with size seemed bizarre to me, but I saw it everywhere. When I would tell strangers what I did for a living, they would predictably first (a) squeal with delight, then (b) ask when I was opening another Homeroom. Surely because I had one successful restaurant, another one must be all I wanted, right? If one is great, two must be double great! And if you can be everywhere in America, even better! But what if I didn't want another one?

In my experience, the closest thing to having a business is having a child. My business is a complex being whose development I am deeply invested in and my worry about it keeps me up at night. Both my kids and my company represent my largest investment of time and money, and each took considerable time, effort, and love to gestate and bring into the world. Embarrassingly, I have read many more books about business than I have about parenting.

While my two kids are the loves of my life, it would be downright bonkers to grade my success as a parent by how many children I have. I can't imagine scanning shelves of parenting books and being confronted by an onslaught of volumes trying to convince people to be good parents by having the biggest family possible. My apologies in advance to Mormons and Catholics, but the only parenting philosophies I see being sold along these lines are highly hierarchical religious traditions led by white men. To the rest of us, most women included, I am guessing that parenting success is not a numbers game.

As a parent of two kids, I can also say two is *not* double the greatness of one. It is double the love, but somehow three times as hard, and quadruple as exhausting as having just one. I define my success as a parent by the quality of my relationship with my children rather than by how many children I am able to raise. Similarly, I defined the success of my company by the quality of our food, by our relationship with our community, and by being a great place to work. If we served the same number of people every year but were crushing it on quality and community and profitability, I don't think I would ever have felt like a failure. So why were complete strangers asking me about growth, and every damn business book focusing on it like it's such an obvious and universal goal?

I picked up a book that was still about growth, but that at least talked about an interesting way to get there. It was the story of (who else?) a white man who purchased a manufacturing company that was on the verge of bankruptcy. In order to bring the company back to life, the new owner decided to share its dire financials with the employees to spur them into action. Spur them it did, because they were living in small-town Missouri and would be absolutely fucked if this plant closed down. They all collaborated and worked their asses off to get the company out of hot water and make it profitable again. The company put up a scoreboard that they gathered around every week in a meeting, and different employees were responsible for tracking different metrics and talking about them. One person would talk about sales and put the weekly number on the scoreboard. Another employee tracked waste, while a third would track inventory numbers, and so on. Each employee would not just write the number on the scoreboard, but talk meaningfully about what was happening with it. For example, by reducing the inventory on the shelves and not buying as much to replace it, there was less money sitting on shelves and more in the bank. By having all the employees engaged like this, the company was able to make hundreds of small, incremental improvements that added up to make a huge difference.

The author compared business to a game and argued that you could not possibly expect a team to win without sharing with them how they are doing, and a business is no different. And yet this is how the vast majority of businesses are run. I found this compelling enough to sign up for one of the classes taught by the author and hop the next flight to Missouri.

I defined the success of my company by the quality of our food, by our relationship with our community, and by being a great place to work.

My room at the hotel along the interstate looked out over a parched parking lot with weeds growing up through the cracks in the pavement. Across the way was a Sonic drive-thru and a BBQ restaurant that I had to drive across the street to get to because there was no safe way to walk there. On the upside, the ribs were legit.

My class the next day was held in a bright, fluorescent-lit room in a nondescript office park. The company I had read about had spun off a consulting wing to teach others how to use its system, which it called "open book management." I hadn't been in a classroom since law school, and I was trembling from drinking way too much coffee.

"Welcome everyone," said the teacher. "I thought we'd begin by getting down to business. Our company is holding its weekly meeting to review numbers, and we are inviting you to sit in and see how it's done. We'll spend the rest of the day breaking down what it takes to implement our system in your organization, but there's no replacement for watching how the sausage is made. Let's get moving!"

I gripped my notebook and followed the teacher through a labyrinth of hallways into a giant lunchroom. Dozens of uniform-clad employees were sitting around tables chatting or milling about. A gigantic scoreboard hung from the ceiling in the front of the room, and as soon as a clean-cut man arrived in front of it the room fell silent. "Okay, first up!" he shouted.

"Sales! Two hundred and thirty-six thousand," shouted a burly man whose arms were covered in tattoos. "This week booked sales from that new contract we got, and the sales team is closing in on four new ones in the hopper so I am hoping that future weeks will see that number grow. I am going to predict that sales will be up to two hundred and fifty thousand by next week, assuming one of those new contracts goes through."

"Great. Next up!" shouted the man at the front.

"Labor," said a woman in the back, at the top of her voice. "We ran a 28 percent labor cost last week, because we had a ton of new trainees that we were working with. That number is fairly high, so I'm going to predict that for next week it will be back to a more normal 25 percent since we don't have any trainings lined up."

As different employees shared the numbers that they tracked, the story behind the number, and their prediction for the following week, it felt sort of like the meetings I sat in with my accountant every month to review Homeroom's financials, except instead of one guy talking at me there was an entire room of people highlighting different metrics. The energy in the room was also considerably livelier than my meetings with my accountant.

The meeting was very, very mathy, with everything from customer satisfaction to employee turnover reduced to a number. As someone who hates math with the intensity of a thousand suns and assumes that all wise people do, too, I was impressed by the level of engagement in the room. People seemed to be actually having a good time in this meeting, becoming animated when it was their turn to speak, and making silly jokes about banal accounting terms. It was inspiring to see someone who had been welding widgets ten minutes ago talk meaningfully about net promoter scores in front of a room full of people. I loved that the format required everyone to participate in a meaningful way—no one could just hang back and watch. As each person in the room came alive to share their number, and their story behind that number, a complete picture emerged as to the health of the business that week, with dozens of little insights into the direction it was headed.

After the meeting, the instructor brought us back into the classroom.

"So," he said, searching the room, "I would love your thoughts and your questions."

I raised my hand. "I thought that was really inspiring."

"Glad to hear it," he smiled. "Joni?"

A woman in the back stood up to speak. "I just loved how everyone was so knowledgeable about such challenging financial concepts."

"Agreed," said a man next to her.

"Bill?" the instructor motioned at a man with his hand raised.

"I thought it was really interesting, but aren't you worried about sharing so much financial information with your staff? Like, couldn't they use it against you in asking for a raise or things like that?"

"That's a great question," said the instructor. "And it's one we get a lot. I'd say the most common fear about using our method is that the information a company provides could be used against it."

Bill nodded his head in agreement.

"The thing is," the instructor went on, "in companies that don't share their financials, employees will often guess at what the company is making. They don't just sit back in their seats without thinking about it—they will just fill in the blank with what seems plausible. And what they think the profit is, is generally much, much greater than what it is in reality. Whenever our system is introduced at new companies, employees are generally startled by how much less the company makes than they had thought. The absence of information doesn't lead to an absence of thought about profitability—it just leads employees to misunderstand it and make poor choices as a result."

I thought about our staff at Homeroom. We would consistently rake in $20,000 in a night, and our staff knew these numbers because so many of them worked the register or took orders. I wondered how much of that they thought was profit. $15,000? $10,000? I imagined they would be shocked to know that the profit was only $2,000, and that is a solid $1,000 higher than the industry standard.

"Other questions?" asked the instructor.

Bill again. "But what happens when the staff finds out about each other's salaries? Isn't that a problem?"

There is always a Bill in the room. Whenever a group is embarking on change, 10 percent of the people will always hate change and will be down on it no matter what. That was Bill. On the other hand, 10 percent of the people in the same group will always embrace change no matter what. That is me. A great mentor of mine once told me that the magic of change has to do with the 80 percent in the middle—the ones who could go either way.

Most leaders focus their attention on the negative 10 percent—trying their hardest to convince them to embrace change. Most of us hear criticism more loudly than we hear anything else, so it is hard to ignore the negative folks. But what happens when leaders spend their time and attention on the negative 10 percent is that the undecided majority starts swinging their way. All of the fears and concerns of this group start sucking up all the air in the room, and folks see where a leader's attention is going and head toward that. The crummy thing is, the negative 10 percent is never going to come around, but in the process of trying to convince the inconvincible, the average folks in the middle start to become negative, too. So even though it's hard as hell, the trick to managing successful change is actually to focus on the 10 percent who are already stoked on change, to focus on building them up, allowing their enthusiasm to infect others, and to help create the momentum and force behind change. When the 80 percent in the middle see time, attention, and resources being lavished upon those who embrace change, and when the conversations tilt toward the positive, they cannot help but be drawn in.

I wondered how the instructor was going to handle this.

"Well, Bill, great question," he said. "I am going to answer it, and then give others a chance to weigh in."

Good call, I thought.

"We don't actually share individual salary information. The point is to provide information that can help people make good decisions. Knowing whether Joe or Jim makes more for their role as supervisor does not help anyone make any meaningful decisions that improve the bottom line for the company. We try to look at numbers that change frequently and that staff has the power to improve, and salaries don't meet either of those goals. So if we look at salaries at all, it is always as an aggregate figure and not with everyone's individual number out there for all to see."

Bill raised his hand again, but the instructor moved on. "Leslie, what do you think?"

"So then where do you draw the line about what to share?" Leslie asked.

"Well that's where the rubber meets the road, as they say," the instructor responded.

I was surprised by how much trepidation was in the room. All these attendees had flown in from around the country to spend a precious week of their lives in cow-town Missouri. They had spent top dollar to sit in this charmless office park presumably because they wanted to institute open-book management in their own companies. However, the level of apprehension over sharing basic financials with employees was palpable.

In my hotel room at night, I stared out at the parking lot and thought about the team I wanted to have, and the kind of game I wanted us to play together. I loved the idea of sharing financials as a way of keeping score together. But if all we did was keep track of financials, then we weren't doing much more than focusing on the same thing as all those uninspiring business books I had read. I called my friend Kate.

"Hey, friend," she said cheerfully, "What's going on?"

"I'm at this class in Missouri," I said.

"Why Missouri?" she replied.

"Just stay with me. Missouri isn't really the interesting part."

"Okay," she said. "Go on."

"So I'm here in Missouri, taking this class on how to use financial transparency as a way to get teams to collaborate on a common goal and measure results."

"Sounds rad," she said.

"It is rad!" I exclaimed. "Except that it feels incomplete."

"Why incomplete?" she asked.

"Because I care about more than just financials. I don't think any of us get up in the morning because we're excited to increase sales. We get up because we're excited to be part of something bigger and more special than ourselves. That thing generates sales, but the sales are more of a byproduct than the purpose."

"So you feel like if you focus on financials you're focusing on the wrong thing?" she asked.

"Exactly."

"Well, why don't you take the voodoo out of it and find a way of putting numbers to the things you do care about. You're making this all sound like magic, but I'm sure it's quantifiable somehow. Just use this system these Missouri people taught you, but make it your own. Like, add the stuff that you care about."

Put numbers to the things I care about. Put numbers to things I care about. I rolled this idea around in my head over and over again. As someone repulsed by math, I did not find it inspiring. The problem is, I knew that Kate was right. My team and I all spoke in abstractions about what made Homeroom special, but how much stronger would we be if we defined success on our own terms and had a way to measure it together? To create a common way to measure our goals, and whether or not we were actually scoring.

"Damn, Kate," I said. "You're good."

18 | Teamwork

It Really Does Make the Dream Work

"A fist is more than the sum of its fingers."

—*Margaret Atwood*

My breath was ragged and shallow as I slung the backpack over my shoulder carrying $70,000 in cash. Inside my eight-months-pregnant belly I was carrying my son, and the extra 60 pounds on my small frame made walking around the block seem like completing an Ironman. Golden Gate Park was pitch black apart from the street lamps, and I tried to wind through the darkness toward my car with alacrity. I just wanted to get inside, lock the door, and speed away.

Homeroom was serving food at a three-day music festival held in San Francisco's Golden Gate Park, fueled by crazy amounts of drugs, booze, and big-name musical performances. Throngs of tech bros, Burning Man followers, and music nerds wound through steampunk visuals, music performances, and tents featuring popular restaurants and breweries. I was Homeroom's ringleader, refrigerated truck driver, and trusted courier for getting the money that we had earned during the day out of the park.

In exchange for access to thousands of new customers and press exposure, the festival took a significant cut of our earnings. This is not that unusual, but what was unusual was that they only accepted it in cash. I did not stop to question how sketchy this was for such a big-name event, and instead decided to accept only cash so that it would be easy to hand over the cut at the end. I did not realize we would be making over $100,000 that weekend.

After doing so many pop-up events before Homeroom opened, my team and I had homed in on how to whip up fresh mac and cheese faster than Superwoman on uppers. We only made one kind—our best seller— the Gilroy Garlic Mac. Gilroy is a California town famous for its garlic, and the dish had been invented by a cook at Homeroom who liked to mix a homemade garlic butter we used in a side dish into her mac every day. The Gilroy got its creaminess from melted gouda, its tangy edge from salty pecorino cheese, and its rich garlic flavor from garlic compound butter (just a fancy phrase for butter mixed with stuff). The result was rich and overflowing with depth despite its simplicity. It outsold the next best-seller two to one.

Most restaurants and food trucks at a festival want to please a wide range of tastes or introduce an audience to different things that they do, so they try to whip up a number of different dishes at scale, assemble them, and get them to customers. By focusing on just one thing, we could churn out food faster than anyone else. Other lines were 100 people deep and moved at a crawl. Ours was 100 people deep and moved like a bar mitzvah conga line. We were able to take an order, collect payment, and get hot food into people's hands, all within eight seconds. I double dare anyone to do better.

We were located off the main stage, where everyone from Phish to Erykah Badu played in the background while legions of staff and friends stirred endless pots of mac and cheese. We had 20 pots going at a time, because our goal was just to have a steady supply of freshly cooked mac to dish out at all times. One row of staff was stamping our logo on compostable bowls, three rows of people were cooking mac, while another would dish up the mac, stick a fork in it, and hand it over to the salivating customer. People loved watching the food be made right in front of them, then heaped into an overflowing bowl and placed in their hands. I'm not sure where they thought mac and cheese came from, but hundreds commented on how cool it was to watch it being cooked. Staff was sweating under bandannas and hats, bouncing their heads to the music, and laughing over the din.

I positioned myself at the front to take orders, in part because I enjoyed meeting our customers but mostly so my giant preggo body could rest on a stool for the day. It is rare to get such immediate gratification watching someone dig into your food within ten seconds of ordering it, and I loved hearing concertgoers exclaim, "Oh my God—this is amazing!" and proudly snap a photo, or devour their dish within feet of our tent. One particularly blitzed customer sat down to eat his mac on the grass, threw up next to himself, and then dug right back in without even moving. Our food was *that* good (and/or he was that high).

The festival attracted all kinds of food vendors, including some of the fanciest restaurants in San Francisco that would come up with a special dish for the event. A Michelin-starred restaurant made porcini-dusted donuts, while a high-end Italian spot churned out crispy porchetta. Other vendors went in a more classic direction with fried pickles, grilled cheese sandwiches, and tater tots. There was an app where you could rate the quality of different food vendors, and despite our Michelin-ranked competition, Homeroom came in at number two out of more than 50 food vendors, with thousands of votes.

Don't get me wrong; there were some serious hiccups. Some staff went on break to see a band play, then never returned. Other staff did return, but came back drunk. Because we were selling so much more food than anticipated, we had to keep placing panicked calls to the restaurant that was an hour away and ask them to send precious sober, non-disappearing staff back to pick up hundreds of pounds of pasta and shredded cheese in their beater cars. And then of course there was the money. I hadn't counted on there being so much cash, and I felt like Pablo Escobar trying to hide it around our tent and then smuggle it out of the park at night. I ultimately started stashing cash in a giant plastic bucket we used to haul pasta and packed it under bags of shredded cheese in the refrigerated truck we had on site. At the end of the evening, I brought my backpack into the truck and stuffed it with bundles of cash, then walked them out of the park hoping that no one noticed.

I couldn't sleep at night having that kind of cash in my house, and I felt afraid to leave my home in the morning knowing it was in there. I was paranoid that someone was watching, or knew it was there, or would rob me on just the day I had hidden $70,000 in my closet. The dark walk to my car every night at the festival was harrowing. My toes would curl tightly in my shoes until they cramped, the hair on the back of my neck prickly.

By the end of the weekend, the stash in my closet was well over $100,000, and $40,000 had to be brought back to the park to give to the festival as their cut. I had to buy multiple cash counting machines, and invited two staff members over to my house to count it all. I felt like some kind of pregnant, dark overlord counting that kind of cash at my kitchen table, and then putting $40,000 in cash into a duffel bag. I drove 40 miles an hour back to the park with that bag in my trunk, praying that I would not be pulled over by the highway patrol.

When I arrived, I joined a long line of vendors waiting in front of the cash-counting trailer. We all looked around nervously, fidgeting with our bags full of cash. I thought that if someone knew about all of this, this scene would make an incredibly easy heist. Hundreds of thousands of dollars in duffel bags protected by nothing more than food artisans is a plotline built for a Hollywood blockbuster.

Inside the trailer, the festival staff had much fancier cash counters than the kind I had at home. It turns out it still takes an awfully long time to count $40,000, especially when your largest denomination is a $20 bill. After it was done, I felt much lighter and breathed a bit more deeply on my way back to the car.

It seemed like the festival was the perfect way to start playing with financial transparency and the system I had just learned about in Missouri. Honestly, I wasn't even sure if we had made any money on it and was genuinely curious. I never believed in paying for advertising, but was willing to do paid events like this one for the exposure regardless of profitability. It would be fun to do an autopsy with the leadership team and figure out whether this one had panned out. The festival was in micro everything we did in the restaurant—guests getting amazing food, staff working and having fun (and misbehaving), a number of drains on what seemed like a lot of money coming in the door.

My leadership team and I had been doing a book club—we were reading a book together and learning about open-book finance, so they had some background in where we were headed. We decided to learn about it and get some experience with it, and then introduce it to the whole company once we had gained a better understanding ourselves.

We went around in a circle and picked different things that we wanted to know about from the weekend. There were basic things like sales, food costs, labor costs, and other expenses associated with the festival. More interesting conversations centered on how to measure staff and guest happiness.

"Could we email all the customers who signed up for our email list and ask them for feedback?" asked Dre.

"Won't all those people be fans? Who else signs up for an email list?" asked Diego.

"Who even uses email?" asked Mick.

"Just people over 50," replied Diego.

Around and around we went until we decided to just keep it simple and use the ratings from the festival's app. We would also measure the average time it took us to serve someone since waiting is universally sucky, and we could use that as a benchmark for future events. In the future, we decided, we could build in more ways to get the kinds of substantive guest feedback we cared about.

As for staff, "We can ask staff to rank their experiences," suggested Ryan.

"According to what, though?" asked Dre.

"How much fun they had?" Ryan wondered.

"But is that really what we care about? Wouldn't the people who went off to get drunk and watch their favorite bands rate their experience really highly? I'm not sure that we will be measuring the right thing with fun," Dre responded.

We decided that fun was a legitimate goal to be measured, but so were a number of other things. We sent staff a short survey on everything from their enjoyment of working the event to their satisfaction with their schedules, with a box for suggestions on how we could improve events in the future.

Everyone on the leadership team picked up a few numbers they would gather data on, and then we would all report back on a large scoreboard at the next week's meeting. We put out slices of peanut butter pie to snack on and toasted with bubbly water before we began.

"To kick us off, I'll report sales," said Dre. She went up to the board and wrote the first number. "$132,000!"

"Holy shit!" cried Maria, our kitchen manager, while the rest of the managers let out a collective cheer.

"I know, I know," said Dre. "We sold more than 16,000 macs over the weekend."

"Jesus," said Diego.

"Guys, this is incredible!" exclaimed Ryan.

Honestly, I was pretty blown away myself. That is what I used to earn as a lawyer in an entire year, and even in my wildest dreams had not imagined was possible to earn in a weekend by selling eight-dollar bowls of macaroni and cheese.

"I know we were all feeling it," said Dre, "that we were running at a crazy pace. Well, we can see it—that number is absolutely incredible. What's wild is that I think we could do more—there were a couple of times we ran out of ingredients because we hadn't prepared to sell that much, so I think we could do more like $150,000 next year if we wanted to."

"I cannot believe we sold that much," said Ryan.

"My feet believe it," said Maria. "I am so wiped."

"Me too," said Diego.

"I'm next," said Maria, walking up to the board. "I gathered information on labor. We spent $52,800 on staff this weekend. It wasn't just the weekend—we had folks cooking all during the week to prepare, and the super-long hours plus travel time out to the event meant that everyone on staff was hitting significant overtime."

"Eep," said Diego.

"Seriously," said Maria.

"I gathered all our other costs for the event," said Mick, walking up to the board. "We had to pay out $40,000 to the festival as their cut of our sales, then another $13,000 in sales tax. We spent $32,500 on ingredients, and another $9,200 on various one-time costs, like the refrigerated truck and table rentals."

"Shit," said Ryan.

"Ugh," Diego let out with a sigh.

As the costs of the event began mounting on the board, and eating away at the gross sales figure, the mood in the room shifted from exuberance to quiet. I walked up to the board to add everything up. "That's $146,700 in costs on $132,000 in sales. So we lost $14,700."

"Oh my God," said Maria, her head in her hands.

"I seriously cannot believe it," said Mick. "That is so fucking depressing."

Everyone looked somber.

"All that work," Diego said, "for nothing."

Everyone paused, staring down at the ground or the table. The room was silent.

"Well," said Ryan, "I don't know if it was for nothing. I was in charge of learning about the customer experience, and people loved us. We scored a 9.8 out of 10 on the festival app with thousands of reviews—only one restaurant did better than us. Staff at the restaurant also let me know that multiple parties came here directly from the festival. Like, they tried Home-room and thought it was so good that when they left the festival, they drove an hour to get here and eat dinner."

"No way?!" said Maria.

"I love that," I said.

The dark mood in the room began to brighten, just a bit. Ryan stepped down from the board, and everyone clapped.

"I also worked on the staff experience," said Dre. "Staff reviews were pretty mixed. Staff who worked the event loved it—they rated it an average of a nine. Many remarked that it was the most fun they have ever had at a job. Staff who worked at the restaurant, however, ranked it really low—an average of a six. We were short-staffed because we sent so many people to work the festival, and they were really feeling the exhaustion,"

Dre stepped down from the board, and took her seat.

"So everyone," I asked, "do you think we should do this again next year?"

"Absolutely not," said Maria. "We lost like $15,000 for a crazy amount of work."

"I disagree," said Dre, ever positive in her outlook. "I think we will earn way more than the $15,000 we lost in increased sales in the coming months from all that great exposure. Plus, I think it was really good for our image in the community based on how much customers enjoyed it."

"And staff really loved it," said Diego. "It was so much fun. I would do it again next weekend. For real."

"I would not," said Maria, sounding exhausted.

"Our customers liked it, but only like half of our staff did," said Dre.

"So do we make decisions around the staff who loved it, or the staff who hated it?" asked Diego.

"I think we could staff more people next year and fix the problem at the restaurant," suggested Ryan.

"That's true" agreed Dre.

On their face, none of these insights was earthshaking, but below the surface, I could see that something important was happening in that room. For one, this team was figuring out what winning meant, and how to do it together.

I thought of all the places I had ever worked. Not a single one had shared its financial information with me, let alone other measures of success. I have no idea if the busy restaurants were making money, or if the law firm was solvent. Most people I know fall into the same boat. That is literally like having a team of blind players running around a field lost, without the guidance of the coach telling them where to go. Normally, my team would have thought we crushed it at the festival and that I went home to bathe in my cash like Scrooge McDuck. But that would have been the equivalent of doing a victory dance after the opposing team scored the winning touchdown. It's a little crazy when you stop to think that most companies operate like this. Instead, I had a team of players understanding that we had lost and already at work on how to win next time.

So why do most companies operate in such a weird way? The reasons for this are myriad and complex, but I think one of the biggest ones is that sharing information and decision-making threatens a very traditional notion of power. Leadership often means knowing the way, having the answers, setting the path. If only you know what that is, then everyone on a team is reliant on you, and you appear indispensable.

Sharing information can make you vulnerable. The information can be used against whoever shares it, and against the company. All of a sudden, upper management is not all-knowing—everyone starts understanding how to be successful, and when your ideas aren't the only ones, they are invariably not always the best ones.

But what you get in sharing this power is so much stronger than what you give away. For one, it builds trust. Over the years, we sometimes struggled getting wide attendance from staff at recess—the weekly meeting where we reviewed all our performance numbers together. The number one reason why: the fact that we were transparent about our numbers and our decision-making meant that staff trusted management more. There was also a lot less pushback to decisions because staff knew they could participate in making them.

Another big benefit of sharing power: it's a lot less lonely. Maybe this seems unimportant, but a lot of people feel this way. A *Harvard Business Review* survey found that more than half of CEOs experience feeling lonely in their role, and 60 percent believe it hinders their performance.[1]

When information and decision-making are not shared widely, it divides people into silos, and it is lonely and high-pressure when you're keeping the numbers and decisions to yourself. I found it a relief not to bear the sole burden of knowing what the fuck was going on, or how to be our best. Based on the energy and engagement in the room, my team found it empowering as well. An outpouring of creative ideas developed for the following year, and our motley crew was starting to feel more like a team.

"So Erin," ventured Dre, looking up from the debate that had emerged on how to proceed next year. "I guess I'm confused. How do we make a decision like whether to do this again next year? Like, do we decide based on money? How much customers loved it? How staff felt? How do we decide?"

> *What you get in sharing this power is so much stronger than what you give away. For one, it builds trust.*

I didn't know the answer, but I realized that I didn't have to. We would figure it out together.

---

[1] https://hbr.org/2012/02/its-time-to-acknowledge-ceo-lo.

19 | Transparency

Essential for the Performance
of Companies and Windshields

"Understanding is a two-way street."

—*Eleanor Roosevelt*

When I went to college, all this public school girl from California wanted was to understand the exotic, preppy world of collegiate New England. I wandered the campus wide-eyed at the ivy-covered architecture, hanging gargoyles, and meandering students sporting boat shoes and shirts with popped collars. I decided to join the preppiest sport of them all, crew, to be at the epicenter of the Talbots catalog I now called home.

I don't know why crew is called crew, but all it is a sport where people row long, skinny boats down a river. It was one of the only sports at the school where the team was not composed entirely of recruited athletes, mostly because only a few elite high schools around the country even have crew teams, given the cost of the sport. You need a boathouse to house and launch an array of expensive boats, rowing machines, and, of course, a nearby river to practice in. Due to the barriers to entry, crew remains the province of the extremely wealthy.

The first few weeks of practice were intended to weed out the weak and the lazy. Practices were held before sunrise so that those who prioritized partying (or sleeping) wouldn't make the cut. Routines on the rowing machines were so taxing that athletes would frequently throw up from the exertion. I wasn't in love with the early wake-ups or the monotony of the rowing machines, but I loved being on the river. Growing up in LA, I had only ever seen the LA river, which is a concrete-lined open sewer designed to take runoff to the sea in heavy rainfall. It is not possible to go in that river, nor would anyone want to even if they could. It is lined with tall chain-link fences and barbed wire, and about as welcoming as Chernobyl.

Rowing Lake Carnegie in Princeton was like being in a postcard. The water was glassy, and it reflected the colors of the sunrise and the shadows from the trees that flanked it. The surface was still until the oars passed through it, sending ripples out to the edges where geese rested. Even though the workouts were grueling, I found the surroundings so soothing it made the rhythmic rowing a meditative practice.

Our coach, Heath, rode alongside us in a pontoon boat, shouting instructions from time to time. I loved the sport, but I couldn't stand his coaching style. He was always putting us down, insulting our work. "Erin, are you even trying?!" he would yell. "Amelia, can you count?"

One day, our boat was really feeling ourselves, our oars moving perfectly in tandem, our speed quickening down the river. Our coxswain, Yashi, the person who sits in the front of the boat giving instructions, was so impressed she was cheering us on as our speed increased. "You all are amazing! You're crushing it!" she yelled at the top of her lungs. Heath, paralleling us in his pontoon boat, raised a megaphone to his mouth. "Stop!" he yelled. "What?" the coxswain asked, thinking she must be imagining things. We were moving faster than ever before—it seemed crazy to break the rhythm. "Stop!" Heath yelled again, and we all dropped our oars, panting.

"Yashi," Heath yelled through the megaphone, "who the fuck do you think you are? A cheerleader? Stop cheering them on and just stick to the instructions you're supposed to give." I was floored. Did he really just stop us because the coxswain was giving us positive feedback? We were rowing the strongest set we ever had, and he pulled us over because of the coxswain's cheering? Fuck this. I didn't need to wake up at the butt crack of dawn each day to be yelled at on a river. I got home and wrote Heath an email saying I was resigning from my position. He replied immediately that if I was going to quit, I would need to do it in person, and gave me the address of his office and a time to meet him there.

My stomach lurched as I walked into the office.

"Take a seat," Heath said. "So why are you quitting?"

"I'm finding the early mornings pretty challenging." I replied.

"Everyone does," he said. "Is that really why you're quitting? You show a lot of promise."

"Honestly," I replied, "I've been struggling with your coaching. Like when you pulled us over to yell at Yashi for cheering us on—I loved having Yashi cheer us on. It felt great. And I just don't know if I want to be part of something where that's not acceptable behavior. Where we have to be so serious or negative all the time."

"Oh," he said, and looked surprised. He paused for a long time. I began to sweat, worrying he was going to chew me out for insulting his coaching style. He had given birth to champion teams—what the hell did I know?

"You know what, Erin," his face softened, "I don't talk about this much, but this year is the first time in my life I've been given the opportunity to coach women. I am so excited to get to do this, but the thing that I am coming to realize is that all those years of experience coaching men are not translating well with women."

"What do you mean?" I asked.

"In a nutshell," he said, "with men, when you yell something like, 'You suck!' they get fired up and work harder—they want to prove to you that they don't suck. With women, when you yell, 'You suck!' they are like, 'Oh gosh, I suck,' and they give up."

He let out a sigh.

"I was trained in a school of thought where insults and negative feedback provoke high performance, but I don't see it working with the women on the team—it just seems alienating. You're not the first female rower to tell me this, and I'm sorry. I was trying to do the best for you, but I think I'm going to need to learn a new way of doing things."

Years later I would return to reflect on that interaction with Heath, and the ways that men and women are conditioned to lead and respond to leadership. At the time, our meetings reviewing the restaurant's performance numbers had evolved to became a focal part of the week. We branded the meeting *recess* because it represented a fun break from our normal routine. Normally, everyone was on the floor, helping customers, or cooking and prepping in the kitchen. It's a rare treat in a restaurant to have a meeting where you get paid to sit, take a load off your feet, and be asked to give input on the business.

For managers, recess was mandatory, and all other staff were encouraged to attend and were paid for their time if they did. We would get dozens of beer samples every week from breweries wanting to get into our tap rotation, so we put beer tastings at the end of the meeting, along with potential new menu items, as an extra bonus for all those who wanted to weigh in. We called our oversized scoreboard our report card, and tracked all sorts of metrics related to the health of the business. We had weekly metrics for staff happiness and turnover, guest feedback, food costs, labor, waste, callouts, you name it. Staff came up with new metrics all the time, and whoever would track it would volunteer to do so for at least six months, so that they could get a real understanding of whatever they were watching.

Pretty universally, once we would start watching a number, it would improve. One staff member suggested tracking food waste, because they noticed they were throwing out a number of dishes every night that were made incorrectly. After much sleuthing, staff realized that the problem was being caused by confusing wording on the kitchen tickets, and when corrected, the misfires were cut in half. This saved tens of thousands of dollars over the years and prevented thousands of pounds of food waste.

In restaurants I had worked in, no one was watching this kind of stuff because we weren't expected to. I would get yelled at by chefs for wasting ingredients, but not because I had any idea how much we were going through, or whether waste was a problem, or how any of this held any kind of significance for the business. I honestly just thought the chef was being an asshole, even though I now understand that those kinds of seemingly meaningless decisions added up to significant differences for the restaurant over time. By engaging all our staff in Homeroom's business, it was like we had a small army involved in improving the business instead of a small team of managers.

We added a system for getting tons of real-time feedback from staff every day to get a more complete picture. At the end of the shift, we asked everyone on the team to pass us a "note." It asked them to rate the shift on a scale of 1–10 as the best part of their day, and to provide the key reason for their score. It also asked about any problems or issues, and asked for staff to suggest a solution for whatever they had indicated. At so many places I had worked the managers are the ones responsible for solving problems, but we wanted everyone to be involved—so we always asked for a solution along with every problem that someone brought forward. We noticed that once we started asking for solutions, about half of the problems that people wrote about went away. Turns out it's easy to complain, but much less easy when you're expected to participate in the solution. Not everyone filled out their notes each day, but we would still receive dozens per week, and this gave us a snapshot of how our staff were doing, as well as tons of suggestions for improvement. We would post the changes we made based on staff suggestions in a weekly newsletter, so that staff knew that their ideas actually did make a difference.

The hundreds of small suggestions and improvements that were made over the years added up in a serious way. In our first year in business, we did $1.6 million in sales. By year ten, we were just shy of $7 million out of our shoebox-sized restaurant. Homeroom's financial metrics put it in the top 1 percent of restaurant performance in terms of revenue per square foot. We were small, and extremely mighty. Even a high-performing national chain like Chipotle would have had to invest in opening multiple stores in the same time span to have achieved the growth we achieved out of our one location. All we did was decide to invest in our own people, and in empowering them to make a difference.

Just as importantly, we started being able to capture information about other things that mattered and have meaningful conversations about them. Before we started tracking numbers, we all had a vague sense of being part of something special, but it was very hard to talk meaningfully about it. Now we could say that we had a value for collaboration and actually see if it was true by how many notes were turned in, how many suggestions we received, how many improvements we put into place, how many people turned up to participate in recess. We could also say that we wanted to be the best part of people's day for guests and staff, and measure it every single week for both groups. At so many places I had worked, the mission of the company was something that sat on a wall and felt meaningless, but we had found ways to actively engage the mission and make it feel alive.

Maybe this seems silly. But the truth is that most jobs suck because they are just about the job. It is boring, and frankly, demoralizing to clean tables for a living. But it is fun, inspiring, and dynamic if your job is to be the best part of people's day—if it's your job not just to clean dishes, but to

Sometimes you learn the most about your values when someone steps all over them.

look at every table, and every situation, as an opportunity to make a difference in the quality of a human life.

An easy way to tell if where you work actually cares about its mission and values is whether or not performance reviews are linked to it. Plenty of places say that they stand for one thing, but then evaluate, promote, and bonus their people based on another. That was certainly true of being a lawyer. It didn't matter if you harassed the summer interns or punched walls in anger; annual bonuses and promotions were entirely linked to how much money you made the company. What makes so many jobs so dreadful is the embrace of high-performance assholes. So, instead, we made our performance reviews reflect our five core values—with only 20 percent of the weight being on the technical aspects of an employee's job, and 80 percent of the weight being on each of the four other values. Even if you could whip up dishes faster than anyone else, you'd still fail your evaluation if you weren't engaging in collaboration, being the best part of people's day, and so on.

Of course, sometimes you learn the most about your values when someone steps all over them. A few years into implementing our system of transparency, I hired a new director of operations named Bruce, an industry veteran with more than 25 years of experience. After attending a number of recess meetings, Bruce deemed them inefficient because it takes so long to go around a giant table and have different people write their numbers on a board and tell the stories behind them. So he changed the meeting to where all the numbers were projected on a board overhead and he alone would walk through them. He cut the meeting time in half, but had also single-handedly destroyed its value. Transparency was one of our core values, but Bruce's version of it—where the person with the most power simply disseminates information to everyone else, felt paternalistic and like a perversion of what we were going for. We ultimately amended the value to two-way transparency, so that it was clear that what was intended was an information exchange between management and staff, and not just a lesson from up on high.

I ultimately had to let Bruce go because he was a bad culture fit, but in the process of correcting his well-intentioned fuckups I was able to refine what our values meant so that we could better hire for them, train for them, and promote them in the future.

An easy way to tell if where you work actually cares about its mission and values is whether performance reviews are linked to it. Plenty of places say that they stand for one thing, but then evaluate, promote, and bonus their people based on another.

Around this time, I started attending a lot more conferences. At one, I found myself in a circle with some very big-name chefs, all men, who were talking about their restaurants. When the topic of staffing challenges came up, I interjected about using financial transparency at Homeroom and how engaging it was for our team. It was as though a gravity blanket had dropped from the sky and crushed the energy in the circle. No one cared. The conversation immediately shifted to money, with the men discussing how their various restaurants were performing. I piped up, mentioning our revenue per square foot number. All of a sudden, all eyes were on me. "What did you say?" asked one of them, a chef with his own TV show. "What's your restaurant again?" asked another.

I couldn't help but notice that this was often true when I was talking to men. Earlier in my career, like in law school, I was in evenly gender-split environments—but the higher I rose in business, I found myself to be the only woman in the room all the time. I had honestly not given much thought to how men and women looked at business differently until I couldn't ignore that there weren't any other women around.

I am an awkward spokesperson for my gender, not being that feminine myself. A perpetual tomboy in pants and no makeup, I would rather be playing sports than doing most things. And yet, put me in a room full of business dudes and the conversations they wanted to have look a lot different than mine. To me, financial success was a byproduct of building a culture that I cared about, and to them it seemed to be the main event. I began leading with Homeroom's financials in every conversation, and in every presentation, to be taken seriously, reasoning that culture is cute, but money is serious. The CEOs of most of the companies I met were men, while the heads of HR were almost exclusively women. It was like two different worlds with two different leaders.

I began reflecting again on my time with Bruce. He had so much more experience than I did, but had walked in and started destroying one of our greatest innovations. He was focused on how much time and money it was costing us to have a meeting where a large group of people go around sharing numbers and insights they have gathered. He viewed himself—rather than the group—as the center of information. He created something hierarchical out of something that had been flat, and collaborative. He thought that this kind of meeting was standing in the way of achieving greater financial performance, as opposed to the reason we were achieving financial performance. And he was a he.

I don't think that a woman would never do this, but I wondered if the women who did were so steeped in a masculine culture that they didn't see another way. Like my crew coach, who had been taught that the only way to lead at the top was through methods developed by men, for men, I saw that it didn't seem to work for women at all. It made me wonder what different methods women might come up with if we were around in larger numbers at the top. It made me wonder what would happen, for both women and men, if I started actively cultivating more female leadership at the top of my own little company.

20 | Collaboration

Because Ten Minds Are (Usually) Better Than One

"Ultimately a genuine leader is not a searcher for consensus, but a molder of consensus."

—*Martin Luther King Jr.*

The first time a man touched me inappropriately, I was nine and on a family vacation in Hawaii. We were staying at a big resort—the kind that hosts tourist-exclusive luaus at night and serves frozen drinks in giant pineapples by day. To my great delight, my parents let us order things on their room tab, so my favorite activity became swimming up to the poolside bar and ordering a chocolate banana milkshake. As the bartender flicked on the blender, I would start to anticipate the taste of the chocolate syrup that he would drizzle on the inside of the cup for effect. The cloying sweetness pierced through the chill of the drink, and I loved letting the frozen shards of ice sit on my tongue until they melted into a sugary pool.

There was a private beach at the far end of the resort, where toddlers would carve sandcastles into feather-light sand while parents lay on lounge chairs. I loved wading out to my chest in the deep blue water and jumping along with the rhythm of each oncoming wave. As each wave rolled in, I would jump up—my feet leaving the sand while the water rose up to my neck—the power of the wave passing through me. I would repeat this for hours on end, and fall asleep at night with the sensation of my body bobbing up and down in the waves.

One afternoon, the heat was particularly oppressive and the little beach was packed. Out in the water, dozens of children splashed in the waves while a stoic lifeguard in dark sunglasses presided overhead in a comically high chair. I ran into the water and entered the fray of screaming kids, splashing each other and dunking their heads underwater. A gaggle of adults and kids were out a bit deeper, jumping with the waves as I loved to do, and shrieking with glee every time a set rolled in. I waded out to join them and found a spot in the middle of the fray.

A few small waves rolled through, and my tiny body moved through them easily. I noticed a larger wave on the horizon, barreling toward shore. As it came closer, I ducked underwater to allow it to wash over me. As I held my breath, I felt someone's arms gripping my waist from beneath the waves. When I stood up and opened my eyes, the arms had let go and a man was standing next to me in the water. He was a middle-aged white man who bore an eerie resemblance to my good friend's dad. He had a day's worth of stubble, a small man-gut pushing out under his hairless chest, and he was wearing garish tropical board shorts I had seen on sale at the hotel gift shop.

169

He smiled at me with wide dimples, which made me wonder if it had actually been him. He said nothing, and I told myself that he must have fallen over in the wave and accidentally touched me. I moved over a few feet, as the next set started to roll through.

When the next big wave arrived, I pushed my body beneath the waves only to be greeted by his hands again—this time around my chest. I stood up, stunned. I didn't understand what was happening and was unsure of what to do. I looked toward shore over the teeming crowds in the shallows, the lifeguard staring at the horizon, unmoved. Kids' voices were everywhere, but my head was filled with a deafening silence. I could see another set on the horizon, quickly headed toward me.

When the next big wave rolled through, I tried to move away from the man, hoping against hope that he was just losing his footing and was groping me by accident in the chaos of the charging wave. He moved toward me, though, and this time, as my head ducked under the wave, he grabbed directly at my crotch, trying to pry his hand beneath my bathing suit. I stood up, dazed, as the wave receded.

The world felt like it was spinning, moving in slow motion around me. The man was stoic, as though nothing had happened, just waiting for the next set to roll through. The sounds of children squealing with delight flooded the air, and as I looked around I didn't know how to place myself in this scene that looked so normal, so safe.

I waded out of the water, terrified the man would follow me. I walked up the sandy banks, past the lifeguard, who remained unmoved, and headed toward the pool to find my parents. When I found them, I didn't share what happened—I merely stayed in their range of sight, splashing in the pool with my siblings as though nothing had occurred, watching with vigilance for the man who had touched me to appear at any moment.

I never saw him again, and I never told my parents what happened. I feared that if I told them that they would confront him, and that he would say that I was lying. I don't know what gave me the impression that would happen, but it was a prescient thought for a nine-year-old girl to have about the way these things usually play out.

Years later, I was brought back to this moment, and so many like them. I was sitting by my computer at Homeroom, nursing a white cheddar mac with peas, when a string of disturbing emails began to populate my inbox.

"A big problem," said one. "Need to talk to you," said another. One by one, emails from female staff members began pouring in alluding to a large issue and requesting a meeting with me.

"Fuck," I thought, "I'm getting sued."

We set a group meeting for the following morning in a small office that had windows overlooking a parking lot. We had to keep them shut, because the parking lot was also home to three large dumpster bins, and the stench was overpowering. This lent an unfortunate sweatbox effect to the room under already-tense circumstances, but it was the only private place we had to hold the meeting.

There were only a few seats, so people sat wherever they could—on desks, on the floor, leaning up against the doorway. About 15 women filed in, nervously chattering among themselves. I had spent the night before anxiously imagining what the problem might be, and let my former lawyer brain go to all sorts of crazy possibilities. Had we violated some kind of obscure law? Was someone selling drugs in the alleyway again? The fact that everyone had coordinated their emails to land in my inbox within minutes of each other and demanded a meeting as a group had me conjuring up nightmares of some kind of class action lawsuit (albeit for what, I had no clue).

Two of our most outspoken servers, Felicia and Camila, quickly emerged as the leaders of the group. While everyone else sat quietly, they remained standing, and when I shut the door and asked if we could begin, they came forward.

Camila kicked things off. She was a crisp professional, always remembering regulars' names and their favorite dishes, going above and beyond to add warm touches like a handwritten note on receipts. She had worked at Homeroom for years, and I had tried tapping her multiple times for leadership positions, but each time she demurred. Camila genuinely enjoyed the daily joys of connecting with customers, and Homeroom was one of few places where servers could create change and didn't need to be in leadership to have a voice.

"Thanks for meeting with us today," she said, fiddling with the hem of her shirt. "And everyone—thanks for being here. I know this is kind of scary."

"Of course," I replied. "What's going on?"

"We called this meeting because we have all experienced harassment at work, and we wanted to tell you about it. We have all experienced similar problems at other restaurants, but this is the first one where we thought that someone would care to listen and maybe do something about it."

My mind instantly began racing. I spent my days and nights in the restaurant, working side by side with everyone, running dishes, chatting up customers. I had detected nothing, and yet here were 15 women staring at me with concern. What kind of harassment had I been missing? I was silent, waiting for Camila to proceed.

"This week Mischa had a customer put his hand up her shirt. It was a father, with his entire family sitting with him at a booth. When Mischa reached over to clear dishes, he put his hand up her shirt and touched her stomach."

I looked at Mischa. Her face was ashen, the color drained away. She was fighting back tears.

"When we sat down after shift to talk about it," Camila continued, "we were appalled. Except as we went around the room, we all started sharing stories, and realized that everyone had a story like Mischa's. We had just been keeping them to ourselves, too embarrassed and ashamed to say anything."

The room was silent, until I finally said, "I am so sorry. I had no idea. Mischa, I am so sorry that this happened to you here."

Heads nodded.

"We wanted to share our stories with you," Camila said.

One by one, the women went around the room and described what had happened to them. Some of them were deeply emotional, welling up and crying while they talked about moments like composing themselves in the bathroom before returning to take the order of a guest who had grabbed them. Others were very stoic, saying few words while speaking their pain, and staring at the floor. A few said they were just there for support and shared nothing.

Over the course of about an hour, the room swelled with every kind of emotion—fury and rage over such deeply personal violations that were happening in plain sight, sadness and pain over feeling hurt and scared while at work. With each woman who stood up, my heart ripped open a little bit more. *How can this be happening under my nose, in a place I wanted to feel like a safe haven from all the bad behavior I've seen in the industry?* I wondered.

"Why didn't any of you say anything?" I asked, fighting back tears.

"Well, sometimes we did say things to managers on the floor," Camila said, "but they didn't really do anything."

"What?!" I replied.

"I mean, we love our managers. Like, *love* them," said Camila. "They're some of our best friends and favorite people. But right now most of our night managers are men, and honestly Erin, they just don't get it. Like, they're all well-intentioned, but when we tell them that someone said something like, 'You look good in that shirt,' they fail to understand why it's threatening. They think about it through their own experience, and because they wouldn't feel threatened if a woman said that to them, they don't really get why it's threatening when a man says it to us."

I felt like I had been struck in the head by a bus. We had the most sensitive, lovely men in leadership. These were the kind of guys who were into working for a powerful woman in an industry dominated by men. They were the kind of sensitive, emo guys who cried openly after heart-wrenching breakups, and the kind of gentlemen who would walk staff to their cars at night. If they weren't doing anything, what kind of hope was there for other men? For any men? What was left of my shredded heart sank down into my shoes.

"So what do you think we should do?" I asked the group.

"We were thinking that maybe we could lead a sensitivity training?" Camila said. "Like, teach the men more about what kinds of things we as women experience, so maybe they will respond differently? Felicia and I are happy to lead it."

I noticed my sticky palms unclench. I hadn't been sure what the fuck to do.

"Let's do it," I said, and we made a date for the following week.

Felicia and Camila arranged for everyone to participate in something called a privilege walk. This is the kind of thing that people in red states make fun of Californians for, but there we were. To participate, staff would line up in a row on one side of the room. Felicia led the effort, and would call out a type of privilege. For example, feeling safe walking alone at night. All those who had experienced the privilege would take a step forward. Those who had not would take a step back. In an average room, the chasm between groups spreads very quickly, with white people and men being the farthest to one side, and women and people of color the farthest to the other. The divide between people's experiences becomes visually and physically understandable.

To add context to the activity, Felicia asked for a volunteer at the end of each round to share an experience. So, for example, for those who hadn't felt safe walking home at night, they were asked to share a story of what it was like for them to fear for their safety, or a time when that safety was violated.

This all sounded well and good, except what resulted was an emotional train wreck. Predictably, with each privilege that was announced, the white men on our leadership team took a step forward, and most of the women took a step back. Then a woman would bravely share a story, often breaking down into tears. Women shared stories of rape, assault, being stalked by boyfriends, touched by teachers. In every place that one would like to feel safe—work, school, home—women shared heart-wrenching stories of trauma. As tears streamed down their faces, the men shifted awkwardly in place or stared down at their shoes. They were stuck across the room—both figuratively and literally—unsure of how to respond or offer comfort and staring into the chasm between them and the women.

While I felt that there had been some kind of emotional learning from the day, the privilege walk ultimately resulted in more alienation than empathy and mutual understanding between the groups, and it demonstrated how out of touch the men were with women's reality. The men were clearly horrified at what women routinely endure, but I couldn't see how it made them any more capable of dealing with the kinds of issues we were having at work.

We arranged for another meeting of the initial women's group to discuss the privilege walk and figure out the next steps forward. I lay in bed the night beforehand, thinking about what a bomb the privilege walk had been. I stared blankly at the ceiling as the hours ticked by, my mind busy brainstorming how to avoid another emotional meeting with no clear path out of the shitty woods we were lost in.

The next day we all returned to the tiny office next to the dumpsters. As the women filed in, the energy was different than the first day—more muted. Emotions had been running high all week, and everyone looked depleted. As the leader, I wanted to arrive at this meeting prepared with a solution, or even just some good ideas—but I had none.

Felicia and Camila strode into the office quickly and with purpose, and the spirit of the room lifted ever so slightly. They came over to me and asked if they could begin the meeting by sharing an idea. "I would love that," I said.

Camila walked up to a small whiteboard hanging on the office wall and grabbed a blue marker. A hush fell over the room.

"Some of us have been brainstorming after the privilege walk," she said. "We need an approach to this issue that doesn't involve trying to get men to understand us. That whole experience was so exhausting, and even after we put all our hardest stories and feelings on the table, it felt like they still didn't get it. Even if they had, we can't put ourselves through that every time we want to train new people on the team."

Everyone nodded, murmuring in agreement.

"So we came up with a color-coded system. We think it'll be a lot simpler and easier to understand. It works like this—all a staff member has to do is name a color that

To create anything new of value, you always have to be willing to fail upward, to make mistakes and get a little better every time.

describes a certain situation, and there is an automatic action that a manager has to take. The colors are yellow, orange, and red . . . ."

"There is no green," Felicia said, "because we thought green would be like a green light for harassment, which is not what we were going for."

"So yeah," Camila said, "a yellow refers to a creepy feeling, or a bad vibe."

"A bad vibe?" I asked.

"Yeah," Camila said, "you know, like when you just get a bad feeling. In this case, if you tell a manager, they're supposed to ask what you want to do. Sometimes it's enough to alert them that there is a situation that might become a problem, and other times a staff member might want to have the manager take over the table. It just depends."

"So the staff member gets to choose how it's handled?" a server asked.

"Yes," Camila said. "It's up to them."

"So for instance, if a server feels like a customer is staring at them in a weird way, they can just go up to the manager and say, 'I have a yellow at table two—can you take it over for me?'" Felicia said.

"Okay," I said. "And what happens next?"

"Well that's all for a yellow," Camila said. "The next color is orange. An orange refers to a situation where there's a creepy vibe plus some ambiguous language. So, for example, 'You look good in that shirt.' There's nothing inherently wrong with the statement, but if it's being said by some creepy guy while he is staring at your boobs, you'll feel super-violated. If it's said by a ten-year-old girl, the same sentence might just feel like a sweet compliment. Context is everything."

"So what happens with an orange?" Dominica, our regular Saturday host, asked.

"You report the orange the same way—just saying the color, except this time the manager is required to act. They need to take over the table. The goal is just for this to be a quick exchange of information—something that can happen quickly on the floor, without a staff member having to either relive what they just went through or justify it."

"I love that," Dominica said.

"So now for a red," Camila said, her pace quickening. "A red is like what happened the other day to Mischa. It is touching, or an overtly sexual comment, like 'You look sexy in that shirt.' In this case, the staff member reports the color, just like anything else, and the manager is required to ask the customer to leave."

Everyone was silent. Camila paused for a moment, then kept going.

"We're hoping that this makes everything much simpler—it takes a lot of the tricky judgment calls out of the manager's hands and makes sure that no one has to retraumatize themselves by retelling a story or worry that they will have to justify their feelings about it."

"I love that it honors where everyone is," Alex said. She was a server who had broken down days earlier talking about how a manager had dismissed her concerns about a creepy customer who was commenting on her hair. "Like, my situation the other day would have been an orange, and I ended up crying in the bathroom after the manager didn't do anything about it. Here I could have just said, "orange," not have to tell my story, and had the manager take over the table. I would have loved to just not have dealt with that table, and moved on with the shift. I think this is amazing."

"So are we good to roll this out?" Camila asked. "When can we start using it?"

"Right away," I said.

We made a plan to train the team the following week and roll it out immediately.

"I can't believe we did it," Camila said. "I'm so excited to try this out and see what happens."

"Me too," I said, holding my breath.

To create anything new of value, you always have to be willing to fail upward, to make mistakes and get a little better every time. This philosophy had worked for me with everything from adding new menu items to refining management philosophies. But something about experimenting with people's safety at work felt too important to fail upward. Like I wanted something that would work flawlessly from the start. The problem is, I have never seen another way to invent new things or solve big problems. You just have to be willing to stumble forward continuously. I was grateful for my employees' partnership on this path, but found myself praying at night to a God I didn't even believe in that the road ahead would be a smooth one.

21 | Iteration

Aka Failing Upward

"There is an element of failure in all success."

—*Simone de Beauvoir*

When I was in high school, I ran on the cross-country team. I'm convinced that cross-country is just a funny name for a 3.2-mile race that takes place on natural terrain instead of on a circular track. I am pretty sure the sport originated on the East Coast at preppy schools where students jogged in the woods for their daily constitutional. By contrast, at my public high school in the center of Los Angeles, we would train by running atop an uneven sidewalk that paralleled an abandoned train track. Instead of prancing over felled logs, we would jump over broken bottles and severed railroad ties. Instead of the forest understory, our only shade came from the power lines that towered above, providing the occasional sliver of relief from the beating desert sun. We were interrupted every half mile by stoplights, so it was hard to get an accurate read of our time, or to get into a rhythm due to the frequent pauses for oncoming traffic. The great part about training in such subpar conditions is that the dusty, anemic trail we competed on 45 minutes away felt like a verdant rainforest by comparison.

When I think back to the most challenging parts of those training runs, though, it wasn't the punishing distances we would run after a long day, or the sweltering heat beating off the concrete, or even dodging tetanus with my footfalls. It was the catcalls.

The train tracks were a popular place for workers to hang out, waiting to be picked up by someone needing help with manual labor. Small groups of men would sit on short ledges by the sidewalk and frequently comment when we ran by. "Ooh, hot mama—lookin' good!" they would shout, or "Hey sexy, where you running off to?" I always ignored them, staring straight ahead, hoping that if I pretended they weren't there, they would somehow disappear. My body became vigilant in those moments, tensing up with the sense of danger, quickening my pace to get away from them. Often the men would erupt into laughter, or high five each other—to this day I don't understand why it was a bonding experience to harass young girls, but the camaraderie it created made my blood boil.

At night in bed, I would strategize what I was going to say to them the next time it happened. I would imagine what they would do if I told them to fuck off, or the surprise it would elicit if I paused to punch them in the face. I never did any of these things, but I would revel in elaborate fantasies about what it felt like to have the power to make them stop and enjoy my run in peace.

181

I had not contemplated those high school catcalls in years, but the thought of them resurfaced after we started using the color-coded system at Homeroom. I tried to imagine what would happen when someone who committed a red was asked to leave—someone who had made sexual comments like the men who used to call out to me on my runs.

With those men in my earlier years, my fellow runners and I often feared that they might turn violent or that we would have to call the police if we confronted them. At Homeroom, the opposite happened. These men (yes, they really were all men) who were asked to leave after committing red offenses were generally embarrassed. Awkward. Meek, even. No one had ever called them on their shit, and more than anything, they were surprised. They stumbled over words or stared blankly back at the manager kicking them out, unable to process their surprise before finding themselves on the sidewalk. Some put up low-level bluster, but most would gather their things quickly, eyes firmly on the floor, and walk straight out the door.

All I can guess is that they had spent a lifetime proverbially yelling at women running by, and this was the first time someone had stopped, drawn a line in the sand, and told them they weren't allowed to sit there anymore. Judging by the blank looks on their faces, I could tell they were trying to make sense of a world turned upside down.

Maybe it was just one small thing, at one small restaurant, but after I had spent a lifetime not doing anything about this sort of behavior, it felt cathartic. I could feel a change in me, and a change in my team. We stood a little taller, spoke a little more boldly. There was an energy on the floor of the restaurant that wasn't there before—like a tiny electrical current buzzing through the air.

Of course, it wasn't all rainbows and butterflies. When something doesn't work, there is always the question of whether it's a system problem or a people problem. An example of a system problem is when your microwave breaks. An example of a people problem is when your microwave breaks because some unknowing idiot tried to microwave tinfoil in it. The issues we initially encountered with the color-coded system were most definitely people problems.

When the color-coded system was used as intended, it worked great. The problem was that managers would frequently want to interject their own judgment or opinion in spite of being asked not to. Even though independent thinking is often what we hire managers to do, managers making judgment calls is part of what had led to the problem in the first place, and what we had specifically designed the system to circumvent.

One night there was a table of 20-something-year-old men who were out for a night together, and were obnoxiously rowdy when the check arrived. They all fought with each other over who would pay, when eventually one of them shoved his credit card in the female server's apron, grazing her crotch in the process. Touching a staff member was a clear red, and he should have been asked to leave.

While with yellows and oranges, a staff member did not have to relate what happened, we had learned that with reds a manager needed enough background just to kick the person out. For example, the manager needed to know if the customer had made a sexual comment to a staff member or touched them so they could tell them why they were being asked to leave. It's hard to just tell someone they violated the restaurant's code of conduct but not tell them why or how, or be able to have a conversation if they asked questions. In this case, though, when the server told the manager what happened, the manager was concerned that perhaps the crotch graze had been an accident. "What if we ask them to leave and it was an honest mistake?" he asked. "What if he didn't mean to?"

I have found that people will often put themselves in the shoes of the person they identify with most closely in a situation. In this case, the male manager later explained that he imagined what it would be like to be accused of touching a woman inappropriately if it was unintentional, and that made him feel awful. Out of an abundance of caution related to the customer's intent, the manager let it go and never asked him to leave. Female managers who heard the same story pictured themselves in the woman's shoes and were livid that she hadn't been protected. We needed our solution to transcend this divide—to be applied the same way regardless of who was making the call. The server who was touched was demoralized by the situation, and her complaint made its way to my desk.

The bad news when shitty things happen is that something shitty happened. The good news is if you can learn from it, then you can protect other people from future shitty things. In this case, it seemed like a rule that we thought was clear was actually not clear enough, and our manager's violation of it gave us the opportunity to refine it.

We learned that we had to start teaching our team to manage for impact, and not for intent. The example we would use is a woman with a large, distended belly walking into the restaurant. If a staff member said to her warmly, "Congratulations. When are you due?" and she answered, "I'm not pregnant," even though the intent was positive (to make the woman feel seen and congratulated on her pregnancy), the impact would be negative.

When we manage not just harassment but most things, we are managing for impact, and not intent. In the rowdy table situation, it only matters that a staff member had her body touched by a customer, not whether or not the customer was just carelessly exuberant or trying to cop a feel. Sure, one situation feels much yuckier than the other, but in terms of what should happen to the offending customer, it makes no difference. When you are managing for impact and not intent, the guy should have been told that he violated our code of conduct by touching a staff member and been asked to leave.

> *The bad news when shitty things happen is that something shitty happened. The good news is if you can learn from it, then you can protect other people from future shitty things.*

Having the clarity that the system needed to be applied regardless of the intent of the guest made it even easier to use. It also helped managers in a number of other situations, because there is a strong tendency to take intent into account when actually it is impact that matters. For example, when a staff member is late, the impact on the team (having to do the missing person's work for them) is the same regardless of whether the late staff member accidentally missed the bus or is a careless jerk. Sure, we'd rather not have careless jerks on our team—but if a really nice, well-intentioned person can never make it to work on time, does it matter?

After about six months of using the color-coded system, we noticed something surprising happening. Even though we had invented the system as a way of coping with harassment, we found that it was significantly reducing our most egregious incidents. It turns out that very few people just walk into a restaurant and shove their hand up someone's shirt. First, they start scanning for someone they might want to do that to, often checking them out. Then they will test the waters, often with some borderline sketchy comments, and see if they can get away with it. Only after they have gotten a lay of the land and built up some degree of confidence do they attempt something really over the top, like try to touch a staff member.

Because we were changing the balance of power early on in the inter-action, the number of red incidents began flatlining. Most of our staff knew when they were being checked out or were getting a bad feeling that some-one might be threatening. After telling staff that we expected them to listen to those instincts, awareness of cues became the cultural norm, and more staff felt comfortable reporting them. Because staff members began asking for interventions at the level of a bad feeling (yellow) or an ambiguous comment (orange), those situations rarely escalated to the level of an aggres-sive sexual comment or touching. Whereas when we first implemented the color-coded system, almost every female team member reported experi-encing a red, after our first year of using it almost no one did.

The other surprising by-product is that having colors to label behaviors and feelings and actions gave us a common language to talk about harass-ment within the company as well. We had one male manager, Kyle, who loved to exuberantly compliment team members on the floor. "Love your hat!" he would shout, or "Cool band tee—I went to that concert!" One day he passed a female server named Lana and told her she had a great smile, and she reported him.

A line like "great smile" is a pretty classic orange. Sometimes it's meant as a friendly compliment from an old person who has not kept up with the times, while sometimes it's meant as a creepy come-on—like an appetizer to more substantial harassment to follow.

In the average workplace, it might be hard to talk about something like a manager telling an employee she has a nice smile. I doubt it would ever be reported, because it's pretty ambiguous on its face. But because Lana was armed with the language to identify Kyle's comment as an orange, and because she knew that if a customer had said the same thing, she would have asked to be moved out of his section, she knew she should say something about Kyle, too.

I asked Lana if she would feel comfortable having a restorative conver-sation with Kyle to explain why his comment had made her uncomfortable. She demurred. "It's not my job to train him how to be a better human," she said.

Fabulous, I thought, *I guess it's my job.*

Kyle was a white man in his 40s and most closely resembled a human puppy dog in his enthusiastic search for approval. He was always in perpetual motion to try the newest thing or improve upon himself. I got the sense that he was more clueless than dangerous. I invited him to have a conversation with me.

"Kyle," I said, "thanks for sitting down with me today."

"Sure thing," he replied.

"Look, we're here because a team member reported you for telling her that she has a nice smile, and it made her feel uncomfortable."

"Oh my God," he said, "I totally meant nothing by it—I promise."

"I understand. . ." I replied.

"No really" he interrupted, "I promise I wasn't hitting on her or anything like that. I mean, that's awful. I'm so, so sorry."

"Kyle, I'm sure that's true," I said.

"I say nice things to everyone," he said, fidgeting in his seat. "I compliment people's shirts, their hats, their eyes—it's just my way of being nice."

"Kyle," I said, "calm down. You're not getting fired or anything. I'm just here to talk to you about the impact of what you said and figure out some different ways to approach complimenting staff."

"Oh my God—thank you. I was getting so nervous."

"Okay," I said, "first off, do you have any idea why it might not be a great idea to tell a woman she has a nice smile?"

"No," he said, "I thought I was just being nice."

"Okay," I said, "a few things. For one, women are pretty used to hearing that as a softball comment that leads to grosser things. I can't even tell you how many times some random guy on the street has said that to me, and because it seems nice-ish I can't react to it, but then when I remain silent they start lobbing more offensive comments. It's like an introductory line for harassment, so it's much more loaded than you think."

"Okay," he said, "got it."

"Second," I said, "and more importantly, women at work do not want to be complimented on their looks by their boss—they want to be complimented on their work. That's what they are there to do—so recognize that and not things like smiles. So, like, instead of telling Lana that she had a nice smile, tell her that she rocked the way she handled a difficult table or a busy night. It will mean a lot more to her, and that's also what we hire you to do."

"I hear you," he said. "That's helpful."

Kyle really took our conversation to heart, and I watched him transform the way he was on the floor with staff. I never received a staff complaint about him again, and he would later thank me for giving him the opportunity to learn and do better.

There are a lot of Kyles in the world—well-intentioned folks who just don't know any better. I understood why Lana didn't want to talk to him—it's exhausting, unfair, and potentially threatening to point out someone's bad behavior—but it made me wonder what would happen if more women felt comfortable talking to men about these issues sometimes. Would we have fewer men making comments from the ledge?

It also made me wonder what would have happened if Lana didn't have an understanding female boss who was willing to talk to Kyle (answer: nothing). Or what would have happened if the servers who invented the color-coded system hadn't had a woman in power to talk to (answer: also nothing). In an increasingly feminist company, I began looking around me and realizing that I sure was surrounded by a lot of white dudes in leadership.

I had never paid much attention to who was in leadership roles and so Homeroom looked a hell of a lot like most companies—with way more men in leadership than women. I decided to start paying more attention.

The biggest problem was that far fewer women applied for leadership roles than men, so I didn't always have much selection. I had asked multiple female servers to explore leadership roles and was often turned down—they often didn't see themselves in management. So I started doing what any good Jewish mom would do—I noodged.

For those not familiar with the *noodge*, it is Yiddish in origin and Merriam-Webster describes it as to pester or nag. And while anyone can nag, the Jewish mother has elevated it to an art form. Just like my mother would not let the inconvenient fact that I was no longer a practicing attorney prevent her from noodging me to become the next RBG, I would not let the inconvenient fact that my staff was telling me they did not want management roles keep me from noodging them into leadership.

When we had an opening on our leadership team, I approached one of my favorite team members, Cal, to see if she was interested.

> *I had never paid much attention to who was in leadership roles and so Homeroom looked a hell of a lot like most companies—with way more men in leadership than women. I decided to start paying more attention.*

"Thanks, Erin," she said, "I am really flattered, but I don't think so."

"Why not?" I asked.

"Well, I haven't ever been a manager before. I'm not sure I have the right experience."

"Were you a server before you started working here?"

"No."

"Well, why is this any different? You'll learn as you go along. Everyone respects you, you have impeccable judgment, and you always set an incredible example."

"Thanks, but it seems like a lot of responsibility. I'm not sure I'd know what to do."

"Would you trust anyone else's judgment on our team more than yours?" I asked.

"No," she said, "I guess not."

"Why do you think someone else would know any better than you do?"

"I don't know," she said. "Maybe they went to school for it or something."

"I didn't go to school to run a restaurant—I had to learn how to do this all on my own, and I think I'm doing pretty well. Sometimes that lack of experience is actually an advantage because you don't come in with preconceived ideas about how things should be—you can see it with fresh eyes. That kind of outsider's perspective is what makes our team special, and you embody it."

"Thanks," she said, smiling.

"I'll tell you what," I added. "What if you just try it out for a month? We can train you, and you see if you like it. If you hate it, we put someone else in. You have nothing to lose, and you would really be helping out the team even if you don't keep it."

She paused, looking around. "Hmm," she said, "that does sound interesting to me." She got up and gave me a hug. "Thanks for believing in me."

Noodge for the win. In the coming years, I noodged a lot, and our leadership team flipped into a majority of women.

Not long after the Cal noodge, I was on vacation at a cliffside inn on the northern California coast. There is a singular, winding road that traverses the knotty cypress trees towering above the jagged coastline. It is a popular route with motorcyclists, and a group of them pulled into the hotel parking lot as I was preparing for a run. Clad in stretchy running pants and a tank top, I was lacing up my shoes when a few of them walked past me on their way to the inn. "Looks like that running is keeping you trim," one of them commented. "Looking good, girl!" said another.

I was silent, the words drained from my mouth. The familiar feeling of anger welled up inside me, the sensation of heat bubbling upwards, flushing my face. I did what I had done on so many runs—ignored it and kept running. Except this time, I didn't want to. Like when I was a kid in my bed at night, I began imagining what I wanted to say to them. Doing mental gymnastics over what words were just the right words to get them to shut up. It was like a chess match in my head—if I say this, how might they respond? If I said that, would they understand me?

When I arrived back at the hotel lobby after my run, sweaty and spent, I saw the motorcyclists seated for lunch at the hotel restaurant. I beelined for the elevators and sought the solitude of my room. I sat on the edge of my bed, thinking about all the comments in my life I had gotten when I was running. I thought of all the times that men had tried to make me feel weak in the moments I was trying to get strong. I got up, walked briskly back to the elevators, and headed to the restaurant.

The motorcycle crew was ten strong, sitting around three large tables that had been pushed together. They were joking loudly with each other as I came near the table. I spotted a man in the middle who was clearly the leader of the pack and had made one of the comments to me.

"Excuse me," I said.

The chatter stopped.

"When I was outside getting ready for my run, you commented on how good I looked. I doubt you would have made that comment to a man, so I was wondering why you said it to me."

The man looked around the table awkwardly. After a pause, he said, "Of course I would have said that to a man."

Some of the men at the table snickered, while others audibly backed him up.

Fuck. In my mental chess, I had not imagined this particular move on his part. And while the leather vests the men wore did strike me as pretty gay, what the man was saying was clearly false and I didn't know what to do with the curveball.

"We would totally say that to a man," said one of his buddies. "Watch what you're accusing us of, young lady."

"You would tell a man you thought he was attractive?" I asked.

"We were just encouraging you to be healthy!" one of the guys responded.

Well, this is a disaster. I paused and took a deep breath. Somewhere deep within me, I knew that I had to pivot. I thought about Kyle and even my dad and all the other clueless men who make women feel like objects without even meaning to.

"Okay," I said to the group, all of whom were staring intently at me by this point. "Let me put it differently. Even if you had said it to a man, I don't know how a man would have reacted, but it made me feel uncomfortable. It made me feel unsafe."

The ringleader—a gray-bearded man in a leather vest, was silent. The look on his face shifted from jovial to serious, and he silenced the groans that were beginning to emanate from the table. He looked me in the eye for what felt like ten minutes, but was probably no more than a second.

"I'm sorry," he said. "I would never mean to offend a lady. I meant nothing by it, but I never want to make a woman feel like that." He stood up to shake my hand. "My apologies, ma'am."

I walked slowly back to my room, my body shaking from the adrenaline and my mind racing. In all my preparation for that conversation (and conversations like it), I actually thought it was pretty unlikely I'd ever get an apology. If you had asked me what my greatest hope was, it was simply to speak up for myself instead of being silent. To break the pattern in myself of letting men get away with treating me as less-than. I figured that if all women could do this sometimes, then slowly, over time, the world would be a different place. If men knew that they would be confronted by women for their actions, the assholes would be less likely to be assholes, and the nice guys would realize they were behaving like assholes.

I almost gave up when they started gaslighting me about making the comments toward men. The interaction was going so sideways that I just wanted to run away. It blew my mind that the thing that had worked was just sharing my feelings. Most guys don't want to be jerks, including those guys. I felt like in my own small way I had made a difference—that those men were unlikely to make comments like they made to me to women in the future. What would happen if I used my voice like this more often? I wanted to know.

22 | Impact

Kicking Ass and Taking Names

"Never doubt that a small group of thoughtful, committed citizens can change the world. Indeed, it is the only thing that ever has."

—*Margaret Mead*

In high school, I kept a super-lame journal. It was hot pink on the outside and had a lock to keep it secret that had long ago broken apart. I wrote about drama with boys, drama with friends, drama with teachers. The usual high school stuff. I was leafing through it years later when I came to a page where my younger sister Alexis had apparently found it and taken it over. This is where it got much juicier. Alexis was only eight years old, but wrote compelling truths about her young life.

Some noteworthy entries:

September 12, 1995: I found this journal in Erin's desk. I don't think she knows I have it. Oh well.

November 15, 1995: My mom got my brother and I matching bed covers (they are striped). Mine is red and Stevo has blue ones. They're ugly. I wish I didn't have to share a room with him.

P.S. Today is Stevo's b-day. I got him some incense (is that the right spelling?) even though I hate the smell of it. I hope he gets me something for my birthday.

November 17, 1995: Today is my b-day! Yay! Today I turned 8! That's my lucky number. Stevo gave me a hug for a gift so I think I am going to take back my gift until he gets me one (I know I am mean!). Erin didn't get me anything but she doesn't have to because I didn't get her anything for her b-day.

Undated 1995: Today Mrs. Douglas smushed the caterpillar. I don't think she meant to, but it was our class pet. It was supposed to turn into a butterfly but she put her hand inside the net thing it stays in and leaned in too far and fell onto it. She tried to tell us it wasn't dead, but we're not that stupid—she had the poor things guts on her hand. I can't wait until I get teachers that aren't killers.

Hugs masquerading as birthday presents, hideous parental choices of room decor, teachers accidentally killing the class pet and pretending things are fine. The thing that struck me most about Alexis's journal entries is that she knew bullshit when she saw it and didn't hesitate to say so. I think I used to as well, but somewhere in the process of growing up, I learned to silence the truth—not to say out loud the things I know are bullshit, because to ignore the bullshit is to do what it takes to survive a world filled with it.

193

As I began acknowledging bullshit and training myself to open my mouth instead of stuff it down, I felt like I was returning to a more primal part of myself. A part that saw the world for what it was with greater clarity, and not just put a gloss on it to make it palatable. And once that door blows open, there's no stopping the wind.

In 2017, a few years after Homeroom started using the color-coded system, the #metoo movement was in full swing. It seemed a lot of women were fed up with ignoring the bullshit and were speaking up, too.

The restaurant world in particular was having a reckoning that no one had seen coming. Restaurants, more than most industries, are fueled by deviant sexual behavior and misogyny in the workplace. Chefs who were famous for their tempers and sexism were finally called out for their tempers and sexism, and no longer celebrated as culinary heroes.

> *As I began acknowledging bullshit and training myself to open my mouth instead of stuff it down, I felt like I was returning to a more primal part of myself.*

On one hand, I was delighted to see a long overdue comeuppance for creepy dudes who abused their power. On the other, I was frustrated to open the newspaper every day and see the spotlight firmly focused on men. Stories detailing the restaurant empires these men had built, what they had done, what was going to happen to them. They say that all press is good press, and men were sure getting a lot of it.

One weekend, I walked to the end of my driveway and picked up the *New York Times*. When I cracked it open, I spotted a #metoo story about a chef named Zack whose restaurant was down the street from Homeroom. Up until this point, I had mostly seen stories about male restaurateurs with large empires of multi-unit restaurants, cookbooks, and TV shows, but Zack's restaurant was about the same size as Homeroom, and his influence (minimal) on par with mine. This was not a famous chef with a nationally syndicated TV show; this was a locally popular chef from down the street. Why the fuck was he getting coverage in the *New York Times*?

That familiar feeling of anger welling up inside me started percolating upwards, and my mind began spinning. I knew that we were doing innovative work at Homeroom, but I always thought that we were too small to matter. I thought the press would only want to cover major players in the restaurant world, not some lady with a mac and cheese restaurant in Oakland.

As I stared at the article, I found my anger gradually morph into inspiration. If Zack was important enough to make it into the *New York Times* as a harasser, surely I was important enough to make it into the *New York Times* with a solution for harassment. I ran to my computer and began writing furiously.

My thoughts and feelings had never emerged so quickly, or so clearly. Time warped and sped up as I detailed the inner workings of our color-coded system and penned a call to action for other women to share their ideas. The years of frustration, of silence, of trial and error, of failure, of awkward conversations, came pouring out of me. I completed the article in about an hour, and I was sure it was one of the best things I had ever written.

Friends advised me to submit to one publication at a time, so I made a list of the top places I would want this article to run. The first was the *New York Times,* because it felt fitting that the newspaper whose article on Zack had inspired me to write my piece should publish a counterpoint. I was rejected.

When the email came in saying my op-ed was rejected by the *New York Times,* I prepared myself mentally to be rejected by the top 20 publications on my list. I told myself to be happy if I could get it to run anywhere. I made peace with submitting it to my synagogue's newsletter if all else failed because at least my mom would read it. Instead, I submitted it to the second choice on my list, the *Washington Post,* and it was accepted within 24 hours.[1]

I whooped around my living room louder than the day I was accepted to college. My (our) story was going to run in one of the most prestigious newspapers in the country. I teared up at the thought that a system that was invented by a collective of women to solve their own problems was going to be read by millions of people. The color-coded system had transformed Homeroom, and I believed it could transform other places, too.

The day the story ran, my sister sent me a link showing that my article was one of the most trending things on the internet. Nestled right between

---

[1]Erin Wade, "I'm a Female Chef. Here's How My Restaurant Dealt with Harassment from Customers," *Washington Post,* March 29, 2018.

a viral video of baby badgers in a hot tub and Beyoncé's latest album was my article on sexual harassment. Do you know how hard it is to get people to care about sexual harassment as much as they want to watch a cute video of baby animals or Beyoncé? Hard.

Rebecca Solnit, the writer and feminist, did a social media post about it. My inbox flooded with interview requests from around the globe. The *Washington Post* named it as one of its most influential stories of the year, along with articles penned by John McCain and Hillary Clinton. I think even my mom was proud (for a few minutes, at least).

Months later I was invited to Washington to testify before the United States Equal Employment Opportunity Commission (EEOC)—the government agency tasked with enforcing harassment legislation in America. I was surprised that under the Trump administration, a government agency was paying to fly a queer woman from California across the country to share a solution to sexual harassment, but it gave me a small glimmer of hope that maybe our government still works. Or at least that its president has no clue where it spends money (the more likely answer).

I was invited to give a seven-minute talk followed by three minutes of Q&A. I obsessed over my presentation, taping myself giving it over and over again until every sentence was polished, every pause measured, every point clear.

I pulled a suit out of my closet for the first time since my lawyer days. It hung awkwardly on my post-baby body, but still made me feel like I was more significant somehow. My hands were trembling as I walked up to the podium, my throat dry. Once I began speaking, though, the story flowed out so quickly it was as though the pressure from my words weighed down my nerves, ceasing their flutter. I had one of those rare moments where I felt weightless and calm, like I was right where I was supposed to be.

Around the room, pens were down and laptops stopped clicking—people were listening. I spoke about how our team at Homeroom came up with our anti-harassment system and why it works. I also talked about how it is not a magic bullet—that there are cultural changes we need to see in American workplaces if we want to see this issue (and many others) improve. Two main predictors of workplace harassment are majority male leadership and strongly hierarchical structures—systems even I had been guilty of reproducing before realizing I had to do things differently to create a truly great place to work.[2] We can't be what we can't see, and I wanted the entire ecosystem we had created at Homeroom to be highlighted and inspire other businesses. I implored the audience to explore empowering employees with systems for transparency and collaboration as we had at Homeroom, and to emphasize the significance of female leadership not just in solving the problem of sexual harassment, but in helping to create positive change in workplace culture overall.

I ended with this:

> The kind of behavior that is just now being exposed has gone on for as long as business has existed, and for just as long, women have been toiling to create different cultures, norms, and paradigms. These are the stories we rarely hear, and it is time they are spoken. Instead of discussing the misbehavior of men, let's start exposing the great work of women around the country to create more inclusive places for us all to work. The revolution we need is not just ousting powerful men behaving badly, but elevating the status of women behaving well. We need to listen to the suggestions of women for how to solve the problems plaguing them, and put them in the position to change their own worlds.[3]

When I was done speaking, the floor was silent. The EEOC went on to publish my testimony and recommendations, and Homeroom's anti-harassment system would go on to be used by companies not just across the country, but around the world.

[2]US Equal Opportunity Commission Chart of Risk Factors for Sexual Harassment and Responsive Strategies, https://www.eeoc.gov/chart-risk-factors-harassment-and-responsive-strategies; Commission for Gender Equality in the Public Sector 2021 Workplace Gender Audit Data Analysis, https://www.genderequalitycommission.vic.gov.au/baseline-audit-report-2021/workplace-sexual-harassment; H. McLaughlin, C. Uggen, and A. Blackstone, "Sexual Harassment, Workplace Authority, and the Paradox of Power," *American Sociological Review* 77, no. 4 (August 2012): 625–647. doi: 10.1177/0003122412451728. Epub 2012 Jul 2. PMID: 23329855; PMCID: PMC3544188.
[3]Testimony of Erin Wade, US Equal Employment Opportunity Commission Hearing, June 11, 2018, https://www.eeoc.gov/testimony-erin-wade-founder-and-ceo-homeroom.

In a full-circle moment, the following week, I did finally make it into the *New York Times*.[4] The same newspaper that had inspired me to speak out with its frustrating article about Chef Zack's creepy behavior was now writing about me, about my team, and about the solution we had created. Knowing that we had invented something that could improve the lives of the one in ten Americans who works in hospitality felt like a staggering accomplishment. We were just one tiny mac and cheese restaurant, but it felt like we were doing something so much bigger.

[4]Alexandra Yoon-Hendrick, "Spurred by #MeToo, a Harassment Task Force Reconvenes," *New York Times,* June 12, 2018, https://www.nytimes.com/2018/06/12/us/politics/eeoc-harassment-task-force.html.

23

Power

How to Have More of It in One Easy(ish) Step

"The most common way people give up their power is by thinking they don't have any."

—*Alice Walker*

In kindergarten, I was convinced that my parents had accidentally misgendered me. I had been given the most Irish-Catholic name a young Jewish girl could be handed: Erin. It literally means Ireland in Celtic—like the punchy saying "Erin go bragh" ("Ireland forever"). However, I didn't know this at the time. All I knew is that in my Jewish preschool, I was surrounded by boy Aarons in kippahs (the Jewish head coverings that resemble coasters). I had never met a girl named Erin. I didn't know that it was kosher to spell it that way. And it was utterly unclear why my parents would give me a boy's name.

I was told with great pride that I had been named after my deceased grandfather, a man named Aaron. My mother would tell me the brave tale of her father's solo escape from the Nazis from his home in a shtetl in Poland. How he escaped the Nazis only to be captured by the Russians, and sent to a labor camp in Siberia. Toiling in freezing temperatures and growing weaker by the day, Aaron escaped the labor camp and made his way on foot across the war-torn landscape. Aaron had only a sixth-grade education, but traded his skills as a tailor in exchange for food and shelter along the route back to Poland. After a harrowing pilgrimage across Europe, he returned to his small town to discover that his entire family had been murdered by the Nazis during his absence.

Aaron rebuilt his life from scratch and found the strength to create a new home, a new career, and a new family. He died before I was born, but everyone who knew him would pull me aside to tell me a story about how his warmth and generous spirit had touched them.

I couldn't imagine a more inspiring namesake, and yet I didn't know what to make of the fact that I was named after a man. It probably didn't help that I wasn't very good at being the kind of girl that the world expected of a child in the 1980s. My mom had to warn me a week in advance of events that would require a dress, so I could mentally prepare myself for a day without my signature OshKosh B'Gosh overalls. I reacted to the color pink the way one might to encountering cat vomit. I could not for the life of me understand what value anyone saw in a Barbie doll.

At one of my Girl Scout meetings, when asked to go around the circle and say why we liked being a girl, I remarked that it seemed like boys got to do more fun activities like sports and camping, so I really wasn't sure what there was to celebrate about this girl business. We were conned into selling cookies and building blingy sashes with badges for lame things like sewing, while the Boy Scouts were learning to build fires and pitch tents without having to self-fund their activities as door-to-door salesmen. This seemed like a shitty deal to me. The circle fell silent, and the leaders awkwardly moved onto the next girl, who undoubtedly gave a more respectable answer.

In later years, I would come to learn that Erin was one of the most popular girl's names in the '80s, but by that time I had already spent years wrestling with what my boy's name meant for me as a nontraditional girl. I decided that it was actually perfect for me, and came to embrace it as a reflection of my identity as a girl who was drawn to things stereotypically reserved for boys, and who aspired to embody the same warmth, perseverance, and grit of my grandfather. Titles, names, labels—these are the words for how we see ourselves, how the world understands us, and how we hold power (or don't).

As I started to gain traction in my career, I hesitated to use words I had seen mainly attached to men, because I didn't see myself in them. I was doing an interview with a reporter for the *New York Times* when she asked if my title was "Chef." "Oh no, I am not a chef," I replied.

Let's pause for a second. I founded a restaurant where I created all of the recipes. I wrote a best-selling cookbook that has been sold around the world. I had worked professionally in kitchens for more than a decade, including as the leader of my own. If I am not a chef, who the hell is one? So why didn't I say yes?

I had a picture in my head that chefs are people (mostly men) who make fancy food—and my restaurant makes macaroni and cheese. I imagined a chef as someone who wears a fancy chef's whites and a toque (those tall, funny-looking white chef's hats), and struts around the kitchen being brilliant and speaking in French. I didn't feel like a culinary genius; I felt like a really good cook who just happened to open a restaurant.

The more I thought about titles that I felt comfortable using, the more I noticed that I was relying on other people or institutions to bestow power upon me. I had relied on school to give me the title of lawyer, and I was hesitant to allow myself the title of chef without a degree certifying that I was one. I had depended on jobs and bosses to give me titles like teacher or manager, as opposed to seeing those labels as a reflection of the capabilities already within me. Life experiences like learning to cook and starting a business had made me a chef and an entrepreneur, but it was like I was waiting for a voice from somewhere else to tell me I had made it, or to send a piece of paper down from heaven alerting me I could call myself something I already was.

Titles create immediate understanding—they generate reverence. After the *New York Times* interview, I began to realize that if I couldn't give myself a powerful title, then I was preventing myself from recognizing and leveraging my own potential. I was stifling my power, my fullness, my reach.

I was thinking about my role and reading a lot of business literature at the time. The tech world was booming and seemingly every article was about blitz-scaling your lollipop-locating app or how to hire a thousand Polish web developers. Not only did I not identify with these problems, but I didn't identify with the leaders who were being written about. It seemed like every damn leader was a sassy dude in his 20s wearing a hoodie or a Patagonia vest.

I thought that maybe I was just missing something, but when I started doing some homework, I learned that roughly 20 out of the 500 largest companies in America at the time had a female CEO. That's less than 5 percent. That number is a joke instead of a statistic. Even a Pringle is 44 percent potato, and everyone knows that Pringles are not real food.

I wanted to understand why there is more potato in a Pringle than women at the helm of the Fortune 500. I went online and searched "What does a CEO do?" The answer: "CEOs are responsible for managing a company's overall operations, driving profitability, managing the company organizational structure, and creating strategy and direction." Hmm. This sounded exactly like my job. Not only that, but it sounded exactly like the job of so many women I knew—owners of businesses all over Oakland. Some of these businesses employed only one or two people while others employed dozens and made millions. Why didn't a single one of us call ourselves a CEO?

While I couldn't do much for that lousy Fortune 500 statistic, I realized that I could do my part to increase the number and visibility of female CEOs by just calling myself one. At the time I made this decision I had about 50 people who worked with me, but I could have had two and it would have been just as relevant. I set the direction, intention, and purpose of the company, tackled its largest problems, and was the person with the greatest authority. At the end of the day, whatever went wrong, the buck stopped with me, and if the ship went down, I would be the one going down with it. I was the CEO, and had been for a long time.

When you start calling yourself a CEO, people start taking you seriously. I started doing a lot more interviews, speaking at conferences, and became an outspoken figure in my industry. Instead of running a restaurant, I was running a company.

I joined a professional development organization that was only available to CEOs—something I would never have thought to do previously. That organization was composed mostly of men who seemingly had not struggled to give themselves a title it took me years to recognize in myself. The CEO organization provided me with thought partners and mentors on the highest level, and it opened doors to rooms that had been closed to me when I had a different title. One year, I was invited to speak at their annual conference right after the president of one of the largest and most recognizable food brands in the world. We were both asked to talk about building people-centered cultures, and I was freaking out because this guy was a global business leader and I was a lowly mac-and-cheesepreneur.

> *The more I thought about titles that I felt comfortable using, the more I noticed that I was relying on other people or institutions to bestow power upon me . . . . I realized that I could do my part to increase the number and visibility of female CEOs by just calling myself one.*

When I got to college, the dean of admissions said something at the first-year orientation that stuck with me. "When you first arrive at Princeton, you'll look around you and wonder how the hell you got here," he said. "But after a while, you'll look around you and wonder how the hell everyone else did." I have found that to be true time and time again. Not because I'm particularly awesome, but because all people are particularly human. Those overachievers at Princeton still had the bad skin all 18-year-olds do, were socially awkward in a lunch line, and made dumb comments in class when they hadn't done the reading. The president of the gigantic company turned out to be just a normal person with a pedestrian presentation that he had spent much less time on than I had on mine because he knew people would pay attention regardless.

One of his central themes in building an employee-centric business was based on a story of letting a janitor pick the broom he would clean with. No offense, but this was not the riveting message of empowerment I was expecting. By contrast, my presentation crushed. I had practiced it a hundred times in front of a mirror, recording and rerecording to get everything just right. I had a colorful slide deck filled with pictures of staff who had done much more than select their own brooms, with key learnings and takeaways for the audience to use. When I was done, the room erupted in applause and dozens of leaders approached me throughout the weekend to let me know it was the best presentation of the conference.

If I hadn't started calling myself a CEO, I would never have been at that conference. I never would have shared the stage with a global business legend. I never would have realized that I belonged there just as much as he did, or that I had just as much (if not more) to contribute to my peers.

I felt powerful just seeing the title of CEO on my business card. Just as important as how the outside world saw me was how I saw myself with this title. I felt important. Like what I had to say mattered. Like I had power, a voice, authority. The more I referred to myself with a powerful leadership title, the more I allowed myself to feel and behave like a legitimately powerful leader.

I started talking to friends of mine to try to convince them to retitle themselves, calling it the CEO Challenge. There wasn't much I could do about that cringeworthy Fortune 500 number, but I wondered what women could accomplish just by claiming their own power within smaller businesses. Women own about 40 percent of all American businesses and are starting new companies at twice the rate of men, so even if all those women started calling themselves CEOs, it would be a sea change in how we view power.[1] If all those women and moms and aunties and grandmas were CEOs, how might we see CEOs differently?

---

[1] 2019 State of Women in Business Report, commissioned by American Express based on US Census Bureau Data, https://about.americanexpress.com/newsroom/press-releases/news-details/2019/Woman-Owned-Businesses-Are-Growing-2X-Faster-On-Average-Than-All-Businesses-Nationwide-09-23-2019/default.aspx; "The 2024 Impact of Women-Owned Businesses, Wells Fargo Report, https://www.wippeducationinstitute.org/_files/ugd/5cba3e_64800b255fe34eb3b7748e9f953078ab.pdf.

One day I was telling a friend of mine, Mike, who is an executive at a major tech company, about my CEO Challenge. "I dunno, Erin," he said. "I just don't think that small business is ever going to get the same limelight as big business. I mean, all these big companies are driving our economy, employing most of our country. I'm not sure that small business will ever be a big deal."

I went home and transformed into lawyer mode, ready to read up and make a compelling counterargument to Mike (because this is how you get people to change their minds—by fighting with them). I was shocked by what I found. I had thought that on some level Mike was right. I assumed that all of the press attention on giant companies

The more I referred to myself with a powerful leadership title, the more I allowed myself to feel and behave like a legitimately powerful leader.

and even my own insecurity at running a smaller business was because they have comparatively little impact. It turns out the opposite is true.

In reality, most businesses are small businesses. Literally 99.7 percent of all American businesses are small, with 96 percent of all businesses having fewer than 50 employees. Despite most American businesses being small, their collective impact is tremendous. Small businesses employ half of the American workforce.[2] Half! Even in tech, where we worship big players and love to read stories about Google or Facebook, 42 percent of tech jobs are still with small employers. So why the hell was it that every time I opened a book or a magazine I was reading only about huge companies and their techniques for hiring small armies of people? As great as the lessons of Apple or Amazon might be, the insights of those leading on a smaller scale are likely more relevant to the vast majority of American business leaders.

I'm not sure if this is an American thing—like our obsession with SUVs and suburban tract housing—but it seemed like the American "bigger is better" ethos seemed to be clouding our collective judgment about who is important. The myopic focus in press, conferences, and podcasts on leaders of large companies is missing the innovations and insights that might be more relevant to the vast majority of American business leaders. Not only that, but this "bigger is better" bullshit was limiting us to a very homogeneous pool of

[2]US Small Business Administration, https://www.sba.gov/sites/default/files/FAQ_Sept_2012.pdf.

teachers, mentors, and business gurus. I like smart tech bros (and hoodies!) as much as the next person, but by being fed mostly their stories, I was getting an incomplete perspective on business.

I had spent a lot of time thinking about why women weren't better represented in leadership at big companies, which is definitely a problem. But I had not once stopped to think about how powerful small companies are, and that if we take them into account, then women already make up a huge and influential part of America's business leadership. How might we think of business and leadership and power differently if they started appearing in articles and publishing books at the same rate as the leaders of big business?

> *Titles reflect how the world sees us, but more importantly, how we choose to see ourselves— how seriously we take the nature of our ambition and let it manifest in the world.*

If I had waited for someone else to call me a CEO, I would probably never have been one. I never aspired to work at the kind of companies that generally dole out this title and I prefer to work for myself. If I hadn't given this to myself, no one else was going to. And by not calling myself a CEO, I never would have reached my full potential as one. There is a power in titles. There is a difference between someone who takes pictures and someone who is a photographer. Someone who writes and a writer. Someone who leads and a CEO.

While not everyone has the luxury of making their own title, most people have the opportunity to embrace a stronger title somewhere in their lives. Whether that means negotiating a bigger title at work, or just calling yourself a cyclist instead of someone who rides bikes on the weekend, there is strength in titling up.

After discussing the CEO Challenge with my friend Mel, who worked at a big tech company, she decided to try to negotiate a bigger title for her job. Mel had been taking on duties outside of her role for months without asking for anything in return. When someone left the company, she scooped up their tasks. When another person went on leave, she grabbed theirs as well. Mel was painfully bad at asking for consideration, let alone recognition. Her New York–based boss routinely forgot she was stationed out of the California office and scheduled check-ins with her at 5 a.m. She would wake up at 4:30 and take the call in the dark chill of the early morning rather than confront him with the snafu. Mel had been working outside the sphere of her job description for a long time without acknowledgment, and it was beginning to grate on her. The more she looked at it, the more she realized that she shouldn't settle for being under-titled any less than she should settle for being underpaid—both were a recognition of her value.

When we started brainstorming titles together, Mel recognized that just saying certain titles out loud gave her an uncomfortable feeling in the pit of her stomach. Words like "senior" or "director" made Mel feel like they belonged to people older or wiser than she was, as opposed to merely referencing her own role as a person with experience and leadership. The deeper we dug into that gut feeling, the clearer it became that the sensation was her fear speaking. Her shame. Her untapped ambition.

If I had waited for someone else to call me a CEO, I would probably never have been one.
I never aspired to work at the kind of companies that generally dole out this title and I prefer to work for myself. If I hadn't given this to myself, no one else was going to.

After a lot of hand wringing and awkward practice in front of a mirror, Mel ultimately negotiated a bigger title for her job along with a pay bump. When I checked in with her a few months in, she said that she appreciated the increased pay and power at work, but that the biggest shift had been internal. "I feel proud of myself," she said, "and that's rare for me."

Titles reflect how the world sees us, but more importantly, how we choose to see ourselves—how seriously we take the nature of our ambition and let it manifest in the world. I want to see those who have struggled to assert their power embrace bold titles that reflect who they are and what they want to be. I want to see our concept of leadership transformed when the 40 percent of female business owners in America start calling themselves CEOs. And, most importantly, I want the percentage of female CEOs to be higher than the percentage of potato in a Pringle. That's when we'll know we've truly made it.

24 | Purpose

Like Coffee, Without the Crash

"In this life we cannot do great things. We can only do small things with great love."

—*Mother Teresa*

One of the most difficult parenting moments I have ever experienced was formulating a response to a single question from my young daughter Ellie: "Why can't I have ice cream for breakfast?" I initially dismissed the query as the silly daydream of a toddler. Everyone knows you should eat something healthy to start your day off right, so I told her that we were going to have pancakes instead. She responded by asking why we couldn't have ice cream on the pancakes, or after the pancakes like dessert. I was going to have to dig a bit deeper. I had to ask myself what makes ice cream acceptable as a dessert for dinner, but not as a dessert for breakfast? Another unfortunate chink in the armor: Did I, or anyone, really filter breakfast options for their health benefits? When I paused to dissect the content of my proposed "healthy alternative" of homemade pancakes loaded with white flour and butter, I wasn't sure they were actually any more nutritious than a scoop of ice cream.

I struggled to reconcile the widely accepted wisdom that ice cream is not an acceptable breakfast option with the cold, hard truth that I could not find any logical support for this assertion. My philosophy had always been to eat a wide range of foods—some nutritious, some not—that when averaged out, creates something approaching a healthy diet. If you believe, as I do, that dessert is an enjoyable indulgence that is merely one component of a more complete diet, then whether or not you eat ice cream at 6 a.m. or 6 p.m. is completely irrelevant.

In the end, I gave in and served Ellie an oversized bite of ice cream directly from the pint container in the freezer. I gave it to her as an admission that she had defeated my logic, but did so with trepidation, because it felt like I was fundamentally defying a long-held world order. It seemed like a slippery slope toward complete and utter chaos.

Because the answer for why things are done a certain way is generally not based in reason or logic, but in long-accepted habits that society perpetuates without question. And like the prohibition on ice cream for breakfast, I found myself increasingly concerned that the bill of goods I was raised with— the foundation of society as I understood it—didn't make sense.

One of the things I love most about being a parent is the ways it pushes you to constantly question and define what matters in life. It is easy to forget how little we question in the way we engage with and understand the world until a toddler standing in their underwear asks why it is so. And when you start breaking down not just the little things, like ice cream for breakfast, but the big things, like the meaning of love, work, and relationships—that's when it gets really interesting. Because the answer for why things are done a certain way is generally not based in reason or logic, but in long-accepted habits that society perpetuates without question. And like the prohibition on ice cream for breakfast, I found myself increasingly concerned that the bill of goods I was raised with—the foundation of society as I understood it—didn't make sense.

After my *Washington Post* piece came out, my team and I were inundated with interview requests and loads of great press. the *New York Times* ran a large piece about solutions to harassment and featured our system. We were mentioned on NPR, in *Forbes*, in the *San Francisco Chronicle,* and in numerous industry publications. Homeroom became known as a great place to work, and candidates began mentioning our values in their job interviews as a reason they wanted to be hired.

They say that success means getting better problems, and while we were attracting more people than ever who wanted to participate in the business, it was getting very tough to make decisions with so many voices at the table. Also, having built such an employee-centric culture meant that many conversations centered on the employee experience rather than focusing on the customer or the business.

It all came to a head one day with the most mundane of tasks—a review of the holiday calendar. Every year was a bit of a free-for-all in how we decided what holidays to be open or closed for—instead of keeping a consistent calendar, the topic was hotly debated every year to different ends depending on whose voice was the loudest. I knew this was a dysfunctional way to run a business and it was born largely of my own guilt. When you work in an industry that functions as other people's entertainment, it means that your bread and butter is earned when most normal people are at rest. Since my staff spent nights and weekends away from friends and family, holidays felt like an unfortunate collision between high earning potential for the business and high-impact vacation potential for the team. As with Ellie standing there asking for ice cream for breakfast, I needed to find a coherent philosophy to guide our decision-making.

"I think we should be closed this Fourth of July," said Diego. "I have a family BBQ I want to make."

"I think we should be open," said Jose, a worker from the kitchen sitting in on the meeting. "Most of the people in the kitchen need to make money that day—our families depend on it."

"No offense, Diego," said Dre, "But I don't think we should make a decision for our whole team based on you wanting to make a family BBQ."

"Why not?" he laughed. "Okay, but seriously—I bet I'm not the only one. Don't other people have special plans? Want to go see the fireworks?"

"I do love fireworks," said Mick.

"Guys—what about our customers?" asked Dre. "Our mac would totally be the best part of their day."

"Having a holiday off for once would be the best part of my day." replied Diego.

As the conversation devolved into competing arguments, I found myself asking: What should matter the most? Sales? Profitability? Work-life balance? Employee compensation? Guest happiness? Public perception? Having systems in place to measure all the things we cared about was really helpful, but we still needed a consistent way to make decisions using the data we collected—especially when they were at odds with each other. I had been considering the kind of team we wanted to be. Were we merely playing with each other, or at some kind of larger game?

"What if it all matters?" I asked. "What if instead of pitting one group against another, we considered all the groups at once?"

"What do you mean?" asked Diego.

"What if we gave equal weight to the needs of not just the staff, but of the guests, and the business itself, and tried to maximize the collective success of the group? We could measure it and make a decision."

I drew a Venn diagram on the board, with three interlocking circles and a middle area of overlap. "What I want is to make a decision that lands right here," I explained, pointing to the center, "not just in any single area."

"Maybe we could break out into groups and brainstorm for a bit?" asked Cal. "Like, split into groups that represent the team, the company, and the customer? We could all do a little brainstorm session and then present on the needs of that group?"

"Sounds great," I said. "What do others think?"

The group nodded in agreement. "Okay," I said, "let's get to work."

Cal broke the entire team into three groups and sent them off to different areas of the room to collaborate. The goal was for each team to put themselves in the shoes of the group they were representing—the employees, the company, and the customer—and to brainstorm as thoroughly as possible how best to meet the needs of that group alone. The chatter in the room grew loud as everyone got started, and it was punctuated by the occasional outburst of laughter. I didn't put myself in a group, and instead floated to each one to overhear their discussions. Some staff jumped enthusiastically into the exercise, really getting outside themselves and into the needs of whoever they were representing. Other staff seemed to struggle to see beyond their own personal desires and kept asserting them in spite of the instructions. After about 15 minutes, Cal called time and invited all the groups back to the table to share what they came up with.

"Dre, do you want to kick us off with the customer?" asked Cal.

"Absolutely!" replied Dre. "Our group tried to put ourselves in the shoes of our guests and our community, and it was pretty clear that from the customer perspective, having Homeroom be open is a must. Mac and cheese is such a great food for the holiday, and it's hard to imagine why customers would have an interest in us being closed. Also, could we do a special or something, just to make the holiday more fun?"

Cal wrote Dre's main points up on the board under the heading of "Customer" and called on the next group.

"Hey there," said Mick, "my group worked on the employees, and the results were pretty mixed. We started by taking a vote of the employees in our group, and it was split 50/50 between people who wanted to work the holiday and those who would prefer to have it off. Honestly, that made it pretty hard to say what the business should do if it was making this decision from the employee perspective."

"Interesting," said Cal. "But I think for this exercise, you have to take a position. Is that possible?"

"Well, we thought that maybe some kind of compromise position would be best. Like stay open for half the day instead of the whole day, staff it with all volunteers, or introduce holiday pay."

"Thanks, all," said Cal, writing the points up on the board. "Great work. Next up!"

Felicia stood up from her seat and proceeded to the front of the room. "My team worked on the business perspective. We found this a bit tricky because we weren't totally sure what the businesse's interest is. If it is just being profitable, then it seems like being open for the day makes sense. But is profitability the only interest of the business? Erin, we were hoping you could clarify?"

I paused. That felt like a hard one for even me to answer, even as the sole owner. On one hand, if the company is not profitable, then it can't even exist, so that seemed important. But on the other, I couldn't imagine it was in the company's best interest to pursue profitability at any cost.

"If I had to put it into words, I guess I'd say that the company's interest is sustainable profitability. Like, it would be profitable to be open on Christmas because we'd have killer sales, but I wouldn't describe it as sustainably profitable. The impact on staff morale would be so negative that I think it would hinder our ability to retain good people or provide a good experience that day, and in the long run, that would undercut our profitability."

"So, sustainable profitability?" asked Felicia.

"Yes," I said, digesting the hasty definition I had just arrived at.

"Well then, wouldn't that also apply to Fourth of July? Why is that different than Christmas?" Diego asked.

"I think because half the staff actually wants to work on Fourth of July," said Dre.

"I think that Christmas is also a different kind of a holiday," added Ryan, "it has religious significance for so many people. Fourth of July is mostly about having fun. And, we're open for most of the days of the year when it's just about fun. We are people's fun."

"That's true," Diego said.

"So, to put it all together," Cal said, pointing to the center of the Venn diagram, "we should be open on Fourth of July because on balance, it is in the best interests of the company, the community, and the staff. And to maximize the positive impact on all of the above, we can decide if we want to take volunteers to work, institute holiday pay, or adjust hours for our employees. And for our community, we are going to plan something special—whether a dish, or a special event—to amplify our positive impact on the holiday for our customers."

"This was so much better than our other meetings," Maria said.

And thus, collective success was born. After that day, we used this model to help make decisions large and small. Should we stay open an hour later? Should we throw a holiday party? Should we open another location? Breaking a decision down by analyzing its impact on the guests, the staff, and the company made it really easy to understand what mattered, and to whom, and to try to find ways to maximize the success of every group.

We began teaching the model of collective success at new-hire orientations, and so staff began framing questions and suggestions through that lens. About six months into using the collective success model, I had a group of servers come talk to me about changing the language on the menu to increase their tips. To their credit, they did frame it in terms of collective success, even if their reasoning sounded more personally focused. They argued that higher tips would help Homeroom retain better servers, which would translate into even better service for the guests, which would in turn benefit the business. We decided to sit down together and dig a bit deeper, and we invited a few more staff into the conversation. When we reviewed the impact on other team members, the servers realized that higher tips for them would result in an even greater pay disparity between them and other staff, likely increasing tension on the team. For the customer, higher tips would lead to an even higher bill, and it seemed unreasonable to ask the guest to pay more just to increase the compensation of some of our most highly compensated staff. As for the company, it's hard to imagine how higher prices for guests and greater pay disparities on the team would result in increased or sustainable profitability.

After looking at all of that, it became crystal clear to the servers that their ask was not the right choice, and even though they were visibly disappointed, they stopped advocating for it. It was refreshing to have the servers come to this conclusion on their own, even though it was the opposite of what they personally wanted. It was also more productive to go through the exercise together and base a decision on a values set that we all agreed on rather than them asking me for a solution, or becoming adversaries if I disagreed with them. Most significantly, even though those servers didn't get the increased tips they were looking for, not a single one left. It is meaningful to participate in the collective success of something bigger than yourself, and they had faith that this system would ultimately benefit them in the long term even if it didn't at that moment.

At most companies, the decision to be open for a holiday or to launch a new initiative is purely a mathematical one, likely serving a small group at the very top. At Homeroom, once we were able to articulate the goal of collective success, business meetings became a lot more fun, like a game to get more points for everyone. It wasn't perfect—some staff took to this system easily while others were more entitled, and some decisions were much tougher than others—but overall, this shift gave our team a greater purpose, and our game greater meaning. And while I still don't know what to say about ice cream for breakfast, at least we had figured out how to make other important decisions.

25

Meaning

As Fulfilling as Mac and Cheese

"Be yourself; everyone else is already taken."

—*Oscar Wilde*

This story ends roughly where it began—at the ocean, and with a sports metaphor. At the time, I was many years into running Homeroom, into surfing, and into following that little spark from within that grows brighter when I am doing what I love. I had driven out to an aging hippie town for a morning surf and parked my white SUV next to a faded rainbow-hued school bus. I pulled a thick wetsuit over my aging mom body, slipped on a pair of neoprene booties, and slathered my face in the kind of thick, waxy zinc-oxide sunscreen favored by a certain kind of health-conscious parent or, in my case, a pasty-white Jewish surfer seeking maximum sun protection.

I toted my board down to the beach, taking in the sun and the quiet. I spotted a group of surfers near a popular break, and I slipped into the water to join them. As I paddled toward them and their silhouettes became clearer, I noticed something. I had been surfing hundreds of times in my life, but this was the first time all the surfers on the beach were women.

The rules in surfing are simple. When a wave comes, the first person to get on it keeps it all to themselves. This means that as a good wave rolls in, multiple people charge to get on, trying to elbow the other ones out to claim it for themselves. It is territorial, aggressive, and winner-take-all. Like most sports, these rules were developed by men to be practiced largely by men, and for the most part still are today.

On this day, however, there was a brand new playbook. No one in the water knew each other beforehand, but without a word, hundreds of years of tradition were undone and we started playing by completely different rules. We collaborated on how to get the most people on each wave, cheering each other on and celebrating each other's victories as our collective gain.

Instead of competing for the waves, we started sharing them—taking turns. Instead of sitting silently and plotting our next moves, we cheered each other on and celebrated each other's victories. On some waves, instead of taking them completely to ourselves, we would communicate about how we could share them safely and ride them together. It was the most joyful surfing session I've ever experienced, as well as one of the safest. There were no wasted waves, hurt feelings, collisions, or altercations. Surfing had been transformed from an individual to a team sport. Instead of being about individual victory, it became a practice of collective success.

221

This model of collective success spoke to me in a deep way. It made me crave that kind of experience every time I get in the ocean and see the traditional rules as disconnecting and inefficient.

When I look back at the years I spent languishing as a lawyer, or at various menial jobs, the thing missing was the drive toward collective success. I started thinking about why it is so rare to have companies with predominantly female leadership like we did at Homeroom, or why there aren't more female surfers in the water. I believe it is because for many women, like me, traditional frameworks for success just don't fit. Men have long defined the successful work narrative in terms of scaled business achievements and personal fortune, but I was seeking a definition of work success that included connection, collaboration, and collective success. To me, size and profitability were byproducts of other values, and not simply ends unto themselves. I wonder if, like me as a lawyer, more women are not "leaning in" at their jobs because they are not inspired to win at the game they are being asked to play.

That day at the beach encapsulates the gift that I have seen women bring to whatever they touch, but that I had struggled to articulate in my own life and career. And while I don't think that only women can practice it, I believe women are essential to leading the movement. Whether by nature or nurture, I think that the emphasis on communication, collaboration, and care for others accurately depicts the competitive advantage many women bring to the world. Over the years that story became the way I thought about leadership, about defining success, and about my own competitive advantage in business.

When I started to break down the alchemy of what was making magic at work, it looked a lot like what happened in the water that day surfing with that group of women. Instead of everyone keeping to themselves, they were communicating. And the communication was flat instead of hierarchical, traveling between old and young, new and experienced. The two-way

Whether by nature or nurture, I think that the emphasis on communication, collaboration, and care for others accurately depicts the competitive advantage many women bring to the world. Over the years that story became the way I thought about leadership, about defining success, and about my own competitive advantage in business.

transparency we had cultivated at Homeroom looked exactly like this, with ideas, numbers, and problems being discussed between everyone, and our successes celebrated as a group. Our restorative approach to handling discipline was based on similar principles, with a focus on creating group harmony and cohesion over a more traditional model that focuses on the individual.

These values coming together were powerful. Not only was our little restaurant generating top-tier financial performance, but we had created an anti-harassment system adopted by restaurants worldwide, with the power to improve the lives of millions. We couldn't have come up with this groundbreaking idea if the servers hadn't spoken up, if we hadn't collaborated between managers and staff to solve the problem, and if we didn't have follow-up communication at all levels to incrementally improve. If our small team could come together to do this, what might be possible at businesses around the country if we embraced a different paradigm? What would happen if we all came to work with a different and more collective purpose?

On a smaller scale, I was also grateful to discover that I could be one of those people who enjoyed waking up in the morning to go to work, and that it was possible to create a place where other people did, too. There is nothing inherently awful about work as I had feared, but there is something demoralizing for many people about the way most workplaces go about it. This was not perfect— there were many days that straight-up sucked, and many nights when I was sleepless from stress—but overall my worst days at Homeroom were still more fulfilling than my best days as a lawyer.

Creating a more beautiful future of work for everyone is like building a piece of IKEA furniture—the process will be confusing, time-consuming, and leave us with parts we don't know what to do with, but hopefully by the end we'll have a sturdy table for us all to sit at together.

It is my sincere hope that this story provides a paradigm and language for women to understand what is not working in their career or their company, to create something different, and to surprise the hell out of us. I hope it arms women with the language to promote the work they are already doing and gives others a framework for understanding their contributions more clearly. Just as importantly, I want this story to inspire men and nonbinary folks who want to break out of traditionally masculine work roles as well. Not to sound like an arrogant college professor, but the harm of the patriarchy doesn't cut cleanly across gender lines, and the only way this gets better for everyone is if our workplaces (and our world) invite more authentic ways of participating. Creating a more beautiful future of work for everyone is like building a piece of IKEA furniture—the process will be confusing, time-consuming, and leave us with parts we don't know what to do with, but hopefully by the end we'll have a sturdy table for us all to sit at together.

When I look toward the future, my heart swells with hope. We spend more of our lives at work than almost anything else, and I see both older and younger generations asking harder questions about what we want to accomplish while we are there. Who knows what we will be capable of achieving if we make space to keep evolving this game we all spend so much of our days playing? I think we will all work better, learn more, and have a damn good time doing it.

Speaking of having a good time, my daughter Ellie has become a surfer, too. This past summer, she attended surf camp, and on the way there one morning told me that she would be doing a handstand on her surfboard. I laughed her off, assuming she was joking and telling her that was an advanced maneuver even I couldn't pull off. When I arrived to pick her up that afternoon, I scanned the water for her. Sure enough, her board was barreling toward shore with her on her head—her tiny, muscular body upside down as though it was nothing. I felt guilty for doubting her, and for letting what I had experienced limit what I imagined she was capable of. Her younger brother Isaac, who had been excelling at riding waves the traditional way, was inspired by her panache and started trying handstands on the board himself, adding his own flourishes of style along the way.

That afternoon with my children is what I want the next generation of work to look like—filled with innovation, inspiration, mutual respect, and more than a little bit of fun. As the sun dipped below the horizon, I breathed in this moment with them and hoped to witness many more like it in the years to come.

It is my sincere hope that this story provides other women with a paradigm and language to understand what is not working in their career or their company, to create something different, and to surprise the hell out of us.

Epilogue: Mac & Cheese Millionaire

After a decade of running Homeroom, I sold the restaurant in 2020 to a large, venture-backed restaurant company. The acquiring company had some of the biggest names in Silicon Valley as investors, and a seasoned CEO who had led some of America's most prominent restaurant chains. Despite their company being successful in its own right, Homeroom's profitability out of a single restaurant was greater than five of their restaurants put together.

When I started Homeroom, I believed that if I wanted to lead with the values that lit me up, doing so would come at the expense of making money. I believed that financial success was for people who were ruthless, competitive, and winner-take-all. I thought that values like pursuing passion, maximizing collaboration, and sharing success were what led to such bad ideas as communism and John Lennon's albums with Yoko Ono.

What I discovered is that the opposite is true. I learned that by playing a completely different game, I could still win at the one that I wasn't even trying to play.

I never set out to become a mac and cheese millionaire. When I first put together my Homeroom business plan, I had estimated my take-home pay to be $40,000. I was stunned when in our first year I earned more than I had as a corporate attorney. I discovered that wealth generation can be a natural byproduct of creating something meaningful for as many people as possible.

Most of us are raised to believe that getting a big pile of money will solve all our problems and make us happy, but I found the reality to be

225

bittersweet. While I felt gratitude for the financial freedom it gave me, selling my company was like having a kid, raising it for ten years, and then
letting it be adopted by a different family to raise it through adolescence.
Given that I just wrote a whole book about cultivating unique values at
work, you might be wondering why I would sell my distinctive company to
a very traditional one.

The aspirational answer is that I was curious to see if I could initiate
even broader change by influencing this much larger company as a board
member. By having a seat at the table with venture capitalists and famous
businesspeople, perhaps I could make a difference in workplace culture far
beyond the scope of my one small restaurant.

The more practical answer is that I was going through a very costly
divorce, and staring down the barrel of a lifetime of alimony for my ex. After
a decade, Homeroom was a well-oiled machine, and I had also been getting
restless for new work challenges beyond its walls. I had been approached
many times over the years to sell, but this was the first time I even took a
meeting. I knew that a sale would give me an opportunity for a fresh start
in my personal and professional life, but also that you don't get something
new without having to say goodbye to something old.

Changing a company culture is a slow and incremental process. With
new leadership and ownership came a new way of doing things, and what
unfolded was death by a thousand cuts. No huge changes were made, but
when you aggregated all the little things the result was unrecognizable.
Homeroom's operating hours got longer. Its interior was remodeled. Its
staffing models trimmed. People loved coming to Homeroom because it
made them feel special, and the new model felt transactional. While sales
had increased every year for the decade I ran it, we began seeing double-
digit declines within two years of the sale.

Despite best efforts from a veteran CEO and a board I both admire and
respect, Homeroom today isn't the same place that I wrote about in this
book. And while its mac and cheese is still the best in the world, it is a different restaurant and a different workplace than when I ran it.

Maybe this sounds like a bummer of a way to end this story, and in
many ways, it is. To this day, when I enter Homeroom and see signs of shifts
toward a more traditional way of operating, my heart drops. I have cried
more than seems healthy over the loss of structures that I and so many other
people had lovingly constructed. But while this outcome is depressing, it is

also validating. People always told me that it was Homeroom's mac and cheese that made it successful, but I always knew it was so much more. It was something deeper—it was all the ideas in this book. Selling Homeroom proved what I had believed all along—that it was still possible to win by traditional metrics by playing a very different game. Homeroom's financial performance was better running on its unique values with the regular people who built it than it has been with loads of money poured into it and some of the best minds in Silicon Valley trying to improve it.

The other great thing that emerged from the sale is that it helped Homeroom's ideas to spread beyond its walls. A number of employees left and went on to start their own businesses, and have run them in the style of Homeroom. Even those who simply now work for other companies have told me that they bring the ideas and values that we championed into other businesses. Meanwhile, once I no longer had to be at the restaurant every day, I had the time to write this book. I hope it makes you want to use these ideas, too.

If I had one wish, it is that when you put down this book, the thing that sticks with you is a fresh definition of success, one that champions doing something that lights you up and connects you more meaningfully to yourself and your community in the pursuit of something special for all of you. I hope this message resonates in your bones, and that you see these themes in your own life, work, and yearnings. I hope this book gives you the tools to

> *People always told me that it was Homeroom's mac and cheese that made it successful, but I always knew it was so much more. It was something deeper—it was all the ideas in this book.*

evolve your leadership style, or the language to more clearly communicate the type of leadership you have already been demonstrating. I hope my story gives you a way to understand, find, or create the meaning you've been looking for that's been missing in your work life.

If I had two wishes, though, it would be that even if you see these values as soft, or fuzzy, or a complete waste of time, you walk away realizing that you'd better start caring about them even if all you are motivated by are traditional measures of success, like money.

Success for Homeroom was never about how long I would own it or run it a certain way. It was an exploration into whether it was possible to love my work, and how to create a place where other people did, too. On this metric, Homeroom exceeded my wildest dreams years ago. I hope it inspires you to create your own version of Homeroom, whatever that looks like. Whether you are switching jobs, pursuing a crazy idea, starting your own company, introducing collective success at your work, or pushing for a new, lofty title, I hope that my search for love helps you find yours.

Acknowledgments

A heaping, macaroni-filled bowl of gratitude goes out to:

The staff of Homeroom: for being the best part of people's day (particularly mine), for your brilliant collaborations, and for giving so much of yourselves to make Homeroom something worth being proud of.

The Homeroom guests and community: for filling the restaurant with your warmth and love.

Stacey Glick: for helping make this book a reality and for holding my hand on the rollercoaster.

Leah Zarra: for believing in this book unwaveringly and cheering me on every step of the way.

Kezia Endsley: for your thoughtful edits and ideas.

Annie Tucker: for your thought partnership on making this book the best it could be.

Bo Burlingham: for writing fabulous books about great businesses, and for championing mine.

Mary Sue Milliken: for being a total badass, friend, and inspiration.

Gabriela Camara: for your generosity, support, and feeding me the best tacos ever after surfing.

Danny Meyer: for showing the world of business how much they have to learn from hospitality, which paved the way for this book, and for lending your support to my efforts to do the same.

Bob Sutton: for making a business case for kindness, and for living it as well.

Amy Edmonson: for inspiring my own business practices, and for generously using your considerable spotlight to help this book increase its impact in the world.

Peter Knox, Brian Morrison, Alana Whitman, Margret Wiggins, Matt Miller, and the entire Book Highlight team: for caring about my book nearly as much as I do, and working so hard to launch it into the world. Ann Miura-Ko: for your impeccable taste in business and in food, and for taking the time to amplify the impact of this story.

Kathleen Wood, Steven Rosenberg, Will Rosenzweig, Dave Whorton, Peter Stamos, and Ron Johnson: for your mentorship, wisdom, and advice over the years (particularly the tough ones).

Jack, Lisa, Roberta, and the entire family at MAD: for providing a special platform to teach the next generation, and inviting me to participate (and eat).

Ari Weinzweig, Paul Saginaw, and the great folks at Zingermans: for creating an organization that has provided the greatest inspiration and education on my own journey, and for spending your valuable time with me and my team along the way.

Amy Simmons: for setting a great example.

Susan Sarich: for telling me after my first major speech about this topic that I should do this for a living. Your words meant a lot and helped propel me here.

Don Lee: for being an ally, a friend, and my favorite person to dine out with.

The Roomies: for being the best friends and chosen family a girl could ask for. Kreds, Al, Christy, KTJ, Srivs, Spops, Somer, Eb, Jilla, and Teich: I am grateful to grow old spending our Michigan summers together.

Kate Redman: for your wisdom, love, and enduring friendship. Homeroom would not exist if not for your encouragement of me and my weird ideas, and my thinking and life are forever enriched by your presence.

Alex Stiver: for your humor, thoughts on life, and the deepest of hugs.

Kate Jordan: for all the great meals and conversation between bites.

Carrie Feibel: for your thoughtful questions every time.

Erin Patinkin: for lending me your big brain when I'm in a bind.

Meghan French Dunbar: for accosting me in the bathroom that fateful night, and for being my hype girl.

Jennifer Panish: for listening to my problems for all these years, seeing me through some epic changes, and always meeting me with compassion.

Martina Franco and family: for years of love and support for my business and my family.

Stephen Wade: thank you for being my brother and lemonade stand inspo.

Alexis Wade: for being an incredible sis, knocking my socks off with your creativity, and for accepting my calls at all hours.

Nina Simon: for being my book sherpa and my second sister.

Morgan Simon: for being my third sister.

Sarina Simon: for caring for me like one of your own, and giving me pep talks when I've needed them most.

Mom: for being an inspiration, a force of nature, a business icon, and a lover of food—so much of the things that matter to me come from you.

Aba: for always supporting me when it would be easier not to, from my wacky business dreams to the far-flung soccer tournaments of my youth—thanks for being my rock.

Elena: for welcoming me into your life, teaching me about kindness, and making the best fake-out cakes I've ever seen.

Ellie: for the strength of your spirit, the sheer joy you have brought to my life, and for teaching me a thing or two in the kitchen when I think I know it all.

Eliza: for your infectious positive energy, your belly laughs, and for welcoming me with open arms.

Isaac: for the delightful intensity you bring to everything you do and the way your hugs melt my heart every time.

Mav: for being my love, my family, and a true partner in all things.

About the Author

Erin Wade is an entrepreneur, author, and chef whose work innovating business culture has been covered in *Forbes* and the *New York Times*. Erin founded a popular restaurant, Homeroom, which has been featured everywhere from the Cooking Channel to the *Wall Street Journal*. She authored the best-selling *The Mac and Cheese Cookbook,* as well as a viral op-ed in the *Washington Post* about her restaurant's solution to sexual harassment that was named one of the publication's best of the year. Erin has a public policy degree from Princeton and a law degree from UC Berkeley. She lives in the Bay Area with her family and an array of surfboards. Learn more at www .erinwade.co.

Index

Create your own version of success.

Visit **ErinWade.co** and continue your journey to building meaning and connection at work with:

- Articles
- Resources
- Podcasts
- Community
- Engagements
  ...and more!